HAPPY SEXY MILLIONAIRE

ABOUT THE AUTHOR

Photograph by Rick Jones, May 2019

Steven Bartlett is the 28-year-old founder of the social media marketing agency, Social Chain. From a bedroom in Manchester, this university drop-out built what would become one of the world's most influential social media companies when he was just 21-years-old, before taking his company public at 27 with a market valuation of almost £200m.

He was born in a village in Botswana, Africa and grew up as a young black man in an all-white area in the southwest of England. He never had money or good grades, but he did have an unshakeable sense of self-belief and a remarkably unconventional perspective on the world.

Steven is widely considered one of Europe's most talented and accomplished young entrepreneurs and philosophical thinkers.

His podcast *The Diary Of A CEO* has become one of the top lifestyle, business and mindset podcasts in Europe and Steven has accumulated over 2 million followers online.

Dedicated to my mum and my dad. Your love is the reason I survived and thrived. To you, I give all of the credit . . .

and all the blame. x

HAPPY SEXY MILLIONAIRE

Unexpected truths about fulfilment, love and success

STEVEN BARTLETT

First published in Great Britain in 2021 by Yellow Kite
An imprint of Hodder & Stoughton
An Hachette UK company

13

Cover design by Claire Fearon and Anthony Logan

Internal illustrations by Jamie Bryan (p. 43, p. 51, p. 66, p. 80, p. 85, p. 88, p. 96, p. 97, p. 104, p. 112, p. 117, p. 152, p. 153, p. 156, p. 191, p. 210, p. 221, p. 238), Craig Burgess (p. 34) and Jack Butcher (p. 13, p. 17, p. 20, p. 47, p. 60, p. 70, p. 82, p. 89, p. 116, p. 119, p. 122, p. 130, p. 150, p. 155, p. 163, p. 167, p. 181, p. 186, p. 204, p. 243).

A CIP catalogue record for this title is available from the British Library

Hardback ISBN 978 1 529 30149 6
eBook ISBN 978 1 529 39650 8

Typeset in Celeste by Palimpsest Book Production Limited, Falkirk, Stirlingshire

Printed and bound in Great Britain by Clays Ltd, Elcograf S.p.A.

Hodder & Stoughton policy is to use papers that are natural, renewable and recyclable products and made from wood grown in sustainable forests. The logging and manufacturing processes are expected to conform to the environmental regulations of the country of origin.

Yellow Kite
Hodder & Stoughton Ltd
Carmelite House
50 Victoria Embankment
London EC4Y 0DZ

www.yellowkitebooks.co.uk

CONTENTS

INTRODUCTION

I'M A 28-YEAR-OLD black kid from a bankrupt family. A decade ago I was an 18-year-old university drop-out, shoplifting food from the corner shop in an attempt to thwart the throbbing pain in my unfed stomach.

Today, the social media company I founded just listed on the stock exchange, valued at roughly a quarter of a billion pounds. I am sitting on a first-class flight from Sydney to Hong Kong reflecting on how a very normal kid with bad grades at school, who was born in a village in Africa, raised in a bankrupt home, kicked out of school and dropped out of university managed to get here . . . To get here quickly, to get here in love and, most importantly, to get here happy.

I guess the story starts 10 years ago at 18 years old when, three weeks after I dropped out of university after just one lecture, my friend Marc gifted me a diary. On the front page of that diary I wrote the following:

My personal goals:

- 'Technical millionaire' by 25
- Range Rover will be my first car
- Hold a long-term relationship
- Work on my body image

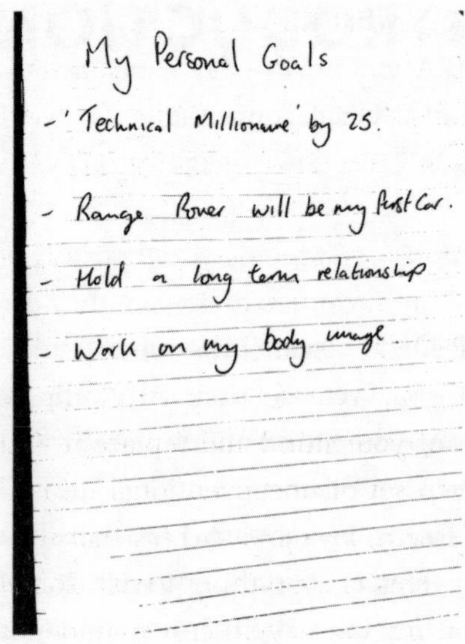

When I look back at this page, I was essentially telling myself that I wanted to be a sexy millionaire by the age of 25, with a girlfriend and a fancy car, and the reason I aspired to be a sexy millionaire is ultimately because I believed that would make me happy.

I couldn't have been more wrong.

Not only was I wrong about how having all of those things would feel, but I was also completely wrong about how you attain those things. This book wasn't written to tell you not to become sexy and rich (I'm honestly a fan of both) but I am going to tell you what nobody told me about these goals, the life-changing revelations over the last 10 years that have made me reconsider everything I thought I knew and, most importantly, I'm going to tell you everything that will ultimately matter more once you achieve all of the above.

If I don't tell you this now, there's an incredibly high chance you'll either never get there, or you'll end up somewhere else thinking you're there and with a series of mental health problems – at least that's what the science says.

I was a victim. A victim of today's media narratives, social media fallacies and societal conventions. Conventions that, if followed, risk leading us down a dangerously miserable and unfulfilling path.

I know that people aren't telling you this stuff because many of them don't have an incentive to do so – they certainly didn't tell me when I needed to hear it the most.

This is a book that aims to suck all of the bullshit social brainwashing out of your mind and replace it with a practical, scientifically proven set of unconventional ideas that will help you find the fulfilment, love and success that we're all craving and searching for. This is everything I wish someone had told me when I started my journey, in easy-to-understand, bullshit- and jargon-free language.

Let me just say . . . I didn't want to write a fucking book. What a waste of time, I thought. I intentionally swerved the publishers and the book agency (sorry, Adrian) for the best part of two years. The social media-obsessed, attentionless millennial in me that no longer valued depth and had no patience would rather have just tweeted or posted an Instagram story to explain my thoughts and absorb the instant likes, retweets and comments, rather than spend years of my life pouring my heart into something so meaningful.

That is exactly why I had to write this book.

I'm writing it as a desperate plea to you – our attentionless, pleasure-chasing, lost, instant gratification-led, mental health struggling generation who are obsessed with money, changing the world, being considered sexy and being happy – so you can tell your followers what you did, be your own boss and have it all . . . Yesterday.

We are a generation that has more information than any other in history but are seemingly further from the right answers than any that have come before; a generation that I genuinely believe are going to be fucked if someone or something doesn't aggressively intervene.

I apologise in advance for every instance where this book offends you. That wasn't my intention but some of the things I believe, and how I say them, aren't always politically correct. There are no ghost writers, no one telling me what I can and can't say here, just my honest uncomfortable truths.

Consider this my intervention.

'HAPPY' (FULFILMENT)

When I talk about 'happiness' in this book, I'm not referring to a mood. I'm talking about happiness in the context of what the word means in our society – an internal feeling of fulfilment. When people ask: 'Are you happy in life?' – they don't want to know if you're in a good mood. They mean: 'Are you fulfilled?'.

In that context, happiness, or the lack thereof, are both extended states; they're not fleeting moods. I can be angry (mood) at someone but happy (fulfilled) at the same time. A mood lives on the surface. Happiness lives deep inside. Our society has told us an appalling amount of lies about how to achieve happiness and what it is. This book endeavours to dismantle the most popular, unaddressed lies that most of us (including 18-year-old Steve) choose to believe and redefine the truth.

'SEXY' (LOVE)

I don't mean sexually attractive (wrong book). Here, I'm using the term 'sexy' as a culturally common phrase to speak to the underlying reason why we all want to be sexy: love; the pursuit of love, the pursuit of becoming loveable, the desire to form romantic relationships and the value that a partner can have in our lives.

'MILLIONAIRE' (SUCCESS)

Again, in our culture, for some reason – probably because of books with titles like this one – becoming a 'millionaire' is seen as a cultural benchmark and measure of 'success'. We've glorified the pursuit; we have shows provocatively titled *Who Wants to Be a Millionaire?* When I say millionaire, I don't mean the attainment of one million £$€, I mean 'success'. Success is a subjective concept based on what you aim for and determined by what matters to you.

This book is about fulfilment, love and success.

Chapter One

DON'T ANTAGONISE THE SPANKER

I RAN OUT of the exit doors of my primary school, looking across the playground through the crowds of shuffling parents, and there she was, stood at the school gates, my 35-year-old mother, with a satisfied smirk sprawled across her face, waiting for me wearing little more than her underwear.

'Fuck.'

On that particular day, my flamboyant African mother had decided to pick me up from school in her bra in order to 'send a (still undetermined) message to the other English mothers'. This is just one story from a library of embarrassing episodes that I dealt with growing up, including the day she made my sister stand in the street for hours holding a sign that read 'I am a thief' after she was caught stealing a cheese string from a supermarket, and the day she decided to give me a bare-arse spanking in front of my childhood crush, Jessica, after I was caught climbing on a roof.

A word of advice for anyone that might find themselves being spanked in front of their first love; it's actually really hard to look 'cool' when your arse is in the air being spanked vigorously by a furious African woman. Also, don't look at your audience. On reflection, I'm sure that my attempts to make eye contact with Jessica to let her know that I was doing okay over here just made the experience more traumatising for her. Lastly, don't act like it's not hurting to seem like a tough guy. That will only antagonise the spanker, prolonging the unpleasant experience for everyone involved.

We were a poor family living in a middle-class neighbourhood in a rural area in the south of England. The youngest of four children, I was a black kid going to a middle-class school full of 1,500 white kids, desperately trying to fit in. The comedian Dave Chapelle once said, 'My parents did just well enough so that I could grow up poor around rich white people'. That sentence resonated with me so much that I can still remember where I was when I heard it.

My mum is black, uniquely colourful, horrifyingly eccentric, firm, loud, overbearing, Nigerian and naturally entrepreneurial – she must have started more businesses than years I have lived: there was an estate agency, a supermarket, a café, a beauty salon, a restaurant, a property renovation business, several hairdressing salons, a few corner stores, a furniture shop, another café, another estate agency. The list goes on. Many of these businesses never saw it past their first anniversary or achieved any real success, and with every new business my mother launched the worse our financial position became as a family. By 2007, it had all come crashing down and I could tell by my dad's stressed demeanour, sporadic and angry comments and his heated arguments with my mum that we were now flirting with total bankruptcy. My dad is the opposite of my mum. He's white, modest, soft, quiet, submissive, English and he's worked the same 9–5 job for as long as I can remember.

We lived in a dilapidated house in a middle-class area. Our back garden was decorated with fridges, VCRs (for you younger ones that don't know what a VCR is, imagine if Netflix was a big box and in order to watch a movie you had to slide a smaller box into it) and other miscellaneous objects littered throughout the waist-high grass. My parents optimistically started a building project when I was seven years old that they never had the money to finish, so the back of our house remained a semi-demolished building site for the best part of two decades.

The front of our house wasn't much better – a smashed window stayed that way throughout my childhood. And the interior of our house looked like a hoarder's dream – broken doors, damaged walls, filthy carpets, rooms crammed to the ceilings with a diverse array of junk, and thousands of my mum's lottery tickets overflowing from drawers.

None of the kids at school ever knew the truth. Not one of my friends ever set foot inside my house in the almost 18 years that I lived there. I always told friends to drop me off at a different house down the road in an attempt to avoid the shame and embarrassment of them seeing the state of our house. I slouched as low as I could in the scruffy, run-down van my dad dropped me to school in, praying that the seemingly unempathetic traffic lights near my school would turn red when I was as far from it as possible, so that I could avoid the shame of being seen in such a contraption.

Despite how hard my parents worked, we never seemed to have money. We never went on holidays, and by my teenage years birthdays and Christmases were apparently unaffordable. On top of this, the vast majority of daily screaming matches between my passionate African mum and my subdued English dad seemed to stem from money issues. At 12 it became obvious to me that having no money was the cause of much of the inadequacy in my social life and most of the animosity in my home life. To me, it was the reason I couldn't have proper friendships or a girlfriend, and why I spent so much of my life acting, living a lie and feeling ashamed, the reason why Christmas Eve was always a rehearsal day for me, the day I practised the lies I would tell my privileged friends about all the Christmas presents I received.

By 14 years old, I had announced to my friends that I was going to be a millionaire. I told my high-school crush, Jasmine, that I was going to 'leave for the city, get rich and come back for her'. Deep down I thought that if I became a millionaire, Jasmine would finally want to be with me. I was convinced that success and money would make me the happiest man on earth. I was convinced they would make me the sexiest man on earth!

So off I went, leaving my small town at 18 years old and travelling to the big city some 300 miles away, with £50 to my name and one clear goal in mind: I was going to become a happy sexy millionaire.

MAKING IT

Fast forward just seven years and I was the 25-year-old CEO and founder of a public company that listed on the stock exchange for some $200,000,000. I had millions in the bank, millions of followers online, I lived in New York and I travelled the world three or four times a week on business. I stayed in fancy hotels, travelled first class and ate the best food. I had the ability to do anything and go anywhere.

Everything had changed. To the outside world I had become that 'happy sexy millionaire' I had always dreamed of being.

But, as disturbing as it felt to admit to myself, nothing had changed inside.

I wasn't . . . 'happier'.

This mind-bending revelation hit me like an unpleasant tonne of anti-climactic bricks at 25 when I found that diary I had written in when I was 18, stating the goals I wanted to accomplish by 25. I had achieved all of them, and ahead of my schedule. So where was the confetti and the marching band, the feeling of immeasurable euphoria and the wave of unceasing ecstasy that 18-year-old Steve had told 25-year-old millionaire Steve he would be greeted with upon arrival?

Someone or something had lied to me.

I felt the same as a rich, accomplished 25-year-old as I had as a confused 12-year-old, longing for birthday presents. I felt the same as a rich, accomplished 25-year-old as I had as a broke 18-year-old university drop-out, living in the worst part of Manchester in a partially boarded-up house, stealing pizzas and leftover food from takeaways to ease the hunger pains. I genuinely was as happy then as I was at 25. How the fuck is that even possible?

All the movies, the Instagram images of rich influencers smiling on their endless holidays, and celebrity culture – they all made me a promise. They had all told me that if you become 'a success' and make bucketloads of money, you will be the happiest person on planet Earth. I felt lied to – lied to by the societal narrative that existed everywhere I looked, and lied to by myself.

The truth is that I was totally wrong about happiness, in every single way. It wasn't until I attained all of the things that I believed would make me happier that I realised some life-changing truths about the true nature of happiness – life-changing truths that made me sit down and write this book.

The first life-shaking revelation that I've come to learn was that I had always been 'happy'. I was happy this whole time! When I was broke *and* when I wasn't, when I was single *and* when I wasn't, when I had no followers *and* when I had millions.

My beliefs about the world led me to believe otherwise, led me to believe that I couldn't possibly be happy yet and that led me to believe happiness was coming, sometime, soon. If I just kept chasing . . .

Maybe you've always been happy, but the world, social media and external comparisons have convinced you that you can't possibly be.

Chapter Two

HAPPINESS IS NOW OR NEVER

THERE ARE TWO kinds of games we play in life: finite games and infinite games.

A finite game is played for the purpose of winning and therefore ending the game, like football, bingo or poker. These games are played within short time frames and they have winners and losers. An infinite game is the opposite. It is designed for the purpose of continuing the play and with the purpose of bringing more players into the game. There are no winners or losers – just an ongoing experience. There is only one infinite game: our lives.

And here is the problem. I spent the first 25 years of my existence believing life was, and playing life like, a finite game.

I saw happiness as something I could 'win' by adding more and more points to some imaginary scoreboard of success, wealth, fame and accomplishment. But how can you 'win' a game when the only end to the game is when the player (you) dies?

Happiness – fulfilment – is an infinite game. You cannot 'win' at being happy. You can only 'be' it, and be it until the player is no longer in the game. In this infinite game, you're not playing within a time frame; the confetti never rains down on you no matter how rich you get and the podium never appears regardless of how successful you become.

UNTIL YOU GIVE UP ON THE IDEA THAT HAPPINESS IS SOMEWHERE ELSE:

- ○ IN A NEW RELATIONSHIP,
- ○ A NEW PROMOTION,
- ○ A NEW DRESS SIZE,
- ○ A NEW SPORTS CAR
- ○ OR IN BECOMING A MILLIONAIRE
- ◉ **IT WILL NEVER BE WHERE YOU ARE.**

It's a perpetual, ongoing infinite experience that only ceases when you die. Because it's constant, you have to play it without expectation of a finish line, without believing in a mountain top and without what I call a 'destination mindset'. All that really matters is now.

Until you give up on the idea that happiness is somewhere else, and that your happiness depends upon any kind of tomorrow – in a new relationship, a new promotion, a new dress size, a new sports car or, in my case, in becoming a millionaire – it will never be where you are.

It's no surprise that philosophers like Lao Tzu frequently alluded to the fact that much of our happiness could be attained just by detaching ourselves from a destination mindset, that living too much in the past or the future would make us miserable. He wrote: 'a good traveller has no fixed plans and is not intent on arriving'. To become a happy traveller on the journey of life, I had to realise that all of these destinations, these milestones and anything that I could 'arrive at', were never going to make me truly fulfilled and happy.

If life was to be an infinite game, and if there was never going to be some magical moment where I 'won', there was this earth-shattering, confusing and somewhat terrifying revelation I had to embrace: happiness is now or never. Despite the influence of social media, society, magazines, marketing and childhood social comparisons working overtime to convince us otherwise, you do not need that promotion, sports car, mansion, Rolex, bag, shoes, followers, that recognition, or external validation. Believe it or not, the liberating and therapeutic truth is that you are already enough.

At the time, these words didn't feel liberating, they felt utterly terrifying, confusing and flawed. What is the point in life then? If I don't have any progress to make, or anything to prove, then why get out of bed in the morning?

I saw happiness as something I could 'win' by adding more and more points to some imaginary scoreboard of success, wealth, fame and accomplishment. But how can you 'win' a game when the only end to the game is when the player (you) dies?

I finally realised that the reason I was playing the game was wholly wrong and the rules I'd been playing by were incorrect and the big trophy I was told I was playing for didn't exist.

IT STARTS WITH SELF-WORTH

This is one of the great paradoxes of happiness: you have to call off the search in order to find everything you've been searching for. Marisa Peer, the world-renowned transformational therapist, had some answers for me. She asserted that:

> 'In 33 years of being a therapist, I've worked with everyone from long-suffering movie stars to anxious Olympic athletes to depressed schoolteachers, and they all have the same problem, they almost always don't believe they're enough. I've worked with thousands of drug addicts and I've never met one that thought they were enough.'

She went on to explain that when someone knows they're enough, they don't lie around doing nothing – in fact, you see the opposite reaction. Knowing you're enough is the realisation of your own worth – which drives people to strive for things even greater than their current circumstance. It's the difference between feeling you need something (often to satisfy an insecurity) and feeling you deserve something (to satisfy your sense of self-worth and your own ability).

No baby has ever been born believing that they weren't enough, no baby has ever held off crying because they didn't feel they were deserving of attention. No baby has ever felt inadequate because of the colour of their hair, eyes or skin. Societal brainwashing, everywhere you look for as long as you have lived, has worked tirelessly to convince you of the exact opposite – that you are not enough.

THIS IS ONE OF THE GREAT PARADOXES OF HAPPINESS:

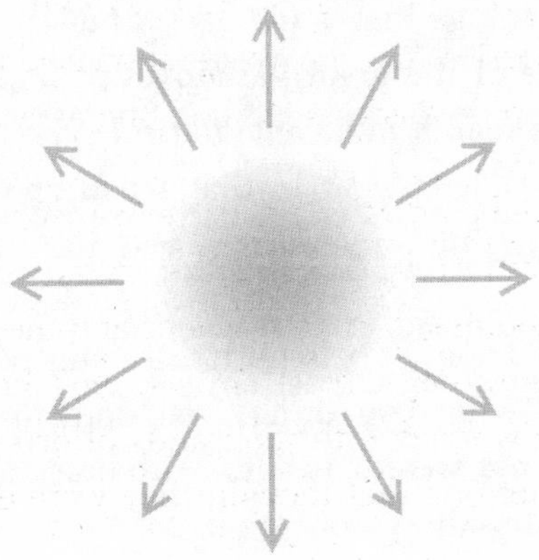

SOMETIMES YOU HAVE TO CALL OFF THE SEARCH

IN ORDER TO FIND EVERYTHING YOU'VE BEEN SEARCHING FOR.

How can corporations sell you shit you don't need if they don't first convince you that there is something you don't have? How can schools and universities inspire you to work hard and climb the corporate ladder if they don't first convince you that there is something up there worth climbing to? How can someone build social status online without convincing others that their life is full of things that yours isn't – but should be?

This is one of the great paradoxes of happiness: we have to call off the search to be able to find everything we've been searching for. The narrative that I had chosen to believe – that I was missing something – was the thing causing my unhappiness.

Social media doesn't help us. It is a status war zone – billions of people showing you things you don't have (possessions, knowledge, fame, wealth, beauty) with braggadocious captions, in the aim of building more status for themselves by doing so.

And the algorithms are on their side. If you post a selfie eating a pot noodle, in bed, looking like death, you will be awarded very few points (likes, reach, comments, followers) by the algorithm. If you post a selfie on a beach in the Maldives, wearing designer clothes, looking skinny, the algorithm will figuratively clap for you, pat you on the back, scream 'well done' and show your selfie to as many people as possible.

People who do this are playing status games, and status games are zero-sum games. In a zero-sum game, you can only gain something by taking it off another person. In social media bragging games, you're gaining social status by 'proving' to the world that you are apparently better, richer, smarter, more successful or prettier than everyone else.

We get a new material possession or boyfriend or holiday and we brag about it to all of our friends and followers to increase our status, and in doing so we're convincing everyone else who doesn't have it that they need it too to achieve the apparent (but usually false) sense of status and apparent (but usually false) happiness that these things have given us.

Social media is lying to you – it lied to me. That sports car, that designer bag, that luxury pile of meaninglessness isn't making people happy; they're playing the wrong game. They're treating life like a finite game.

And if you dare to play that game, you'll spend your life chasing after empty fleeting pleasures, mistaking them for happiness and, just when you think you're going to finally get to where you think happiness appears to be, you finally get that promotion, those millions, that car, the relationship, the fame, it seemingly vanishes. It will seemingly evade your grasp at the last moment, moving further into the distance, like the end of a rainbow.

There's nothing that kills more people than a meaningless life. And the toxic society we live in is slowly urging us to trade meaningfulness for material abundance, followers, likes, isolation and shallowness. They call us the connected generation because of the rapid proliferation of high-speed internet, but the data shows that even in the most densely populated internet-connected cities, meaningful connection is at an all-time low. For 150 years, the life expectancy in the United Kingdom and the United States has increased but shockingly, and for the first time in modern history, it's started to fall. Suicide is now at record rates in the modern era, and addiction is killing more than it ever has.

There's a crisis of meaning in the Western world and it's destroying our lives.

AS OUR INTERNET CONNECTIONS GOT STRONGER,

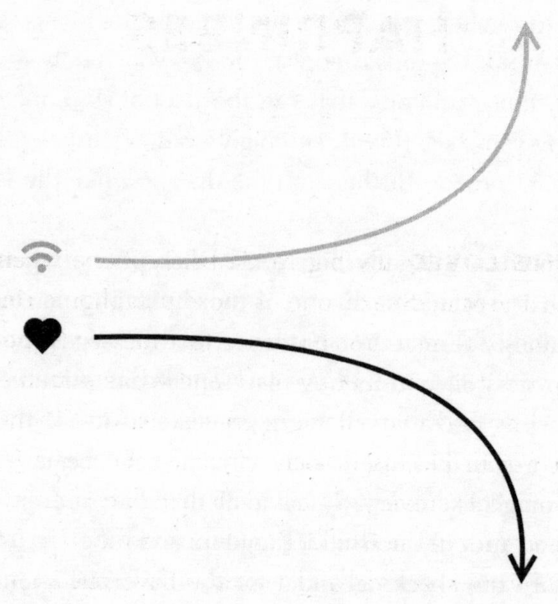

MEANINGFUL CONNECTIONS GOT WEAKER.

Chapter Three

CONTRAST: GREAT FOR SURVIVAL, SHIT FOR HAPPINESS

I FUCKING LOVED my big Nokia brick phone when I was 12. It had Pac-Man, Snake, one of those polyphonic ringtones, and the ability to send 160-character text messages (providing I had topped it up) on its tiny black and white screen – it was mind-blowing and marvellous in equal measure. Owning one made me a 'cool' kid in my social circle at school and I felt like the dog's bollocks every time I pulled it out in front of my friends and proudly hoisted its antenna into the air.

Fast forward a decade and we now have millimetre-thick, ultra-fast, gazillion-megapixel genius phones that perform tasks without us asking them to and that are capable of high-definition video calls from one side of the planet to the other with no delay. My Nokia brick phone is exactly the same as it was then, but if I still had it today I would be deeply embarrassed to own it.

The phone hasn't changed, but the world it exists in has. Isn't it crazy that the perceived value of anything can change with just the introduction of something considered better, shiner, prettier? Think about that – the value the human brain attributes to something can completely change based purely on the introduction of something better – not based on the true and inherent value of the object itself.

One of the great illusions in life is that we are in control of our decision making – that we make rational decisions by weighing up the facts at hand, all of the time. This, put simply, couldn't be further from the truth. A plethora of scientific research has proven that the human mind is deeply irrational and largely driven by subconscious impulses, hormones, survival instincts and the emotions they create.

As frightening as it may be, we are not 'in control' most of the time. Our brains are designed to be incapable of constant rational thought – we simply don't have the time or mental capacity to calculate the statistical probabilities and potential risks that come with the tens of thousands of choices we make every day, so we live largely in an unconscious autopilot state, allowing instinct to be the CEO of our lives.

This CEO is very lazy and a particularly lazy decision-maker. Your CEO makes decisions about your life at lightning speed, usually using a single key factor rather than analysing every tiny detail. Not only is the CEO of your life lazy, they're also a little bit racist, sexist and riddled with other social biases of which you're probably not proud. These biases have been programmed into the CEO that lives in your head based on your past experiences, the media narratives you've been exposed to and your innate desire to survive – after all, when a lion ran towards your ancestors on the savannas of Africa, spending more than a second making a decision on whether they should leg it or not could have had fatal consequences.

As part of their duty to keep you alive, when the lazy CEO

in your mind doesn't have enough information on something, it will make a quick decision based on something called relativity – by comparing and contrasting one thing to another. This means that when your CEO doesn't have enough information, it will make judgements relative to and dependent on the context in which they are presented.

IF YOU MURDERED EVERYONE ELSE, MAYBE JUST MAYBE . . .

Scientific studies show that the choice your mental CEO will make can differ, even when the facts at hand don't change. For example, if a chef puts an expensive steak on their menu it's known to drive popularity for the second most expensive steak on the list. With three TVs on sale at different prices in a store, people often pick the middle-priced option because the cheapest TV is presumed to be a bad choice and the most expensive one to be unnecessarily fancy. The middle price-point is presumed to be the safe and best choice – your lazy CEO is at work with their presumptions again.

Consider this question: would you rather drive 10 minutes out of your way to save £10 on a new £20 jacket? Or to save £10 on a new £200 jacket? The vast majority of us would be more willing to drive the 10 minutes to save on the £20 jacket. But why? Isn't £10 worth £10? Isn't 10 minutes of your time worth the same regardless of the overall cost of the purchase?

Our judgement of the inherent value of £10 seems to change because we determine the value of things relative to the circumstances rather than in absolute and logical terms. We are fundamentally irrational when it comes to fast-track decision making and our assessment of the value of all things. The truth is that nothing in life has any intrinsic value without context.

For us humans, gold is extremely valuable – some people commit crimes and risk life sentences to get their hands on a small piece of the stuff, but to the other 8.7 billion species of animals on planet Earth, it's just a heavy piece of nothing. Within the context that gold is socially desirable within society, we attribute tremendous perceived value to it.

Your lazy CEO loves to make short-cut, comparison-oriented decisions that would have saved you from the jaws of a charging lion 10,000 years ago but, in the context of the social-media oriented world we live in, this approach will inescapably present everyone as being apparently prettier, apparently stronger, apparently sexier, apparently happier and apparently more successful than you, and will almost certainly make you unsatisfied at best. At worst, you'll feel like the worthless inferior and inadequate old brick mobile phone in the presence of 8 billion apparently happy, sexy and rich iPhone owners.

If by some miraculous biological impossibility you were the only person ever born and alive on Earth, you would be free of the physical insecurities, life anxieties and worries about how successful you are or aren't that we're all riddled with now. In your mind, you would already be 'enough' – because you would be the richest, happiest, prettiest, skinniest, smartest, sexiest, funniest, most successful person alive. You would be the standard of 'enough' in every conceivable way.

This is why, as a young kid growing up in a relatively poor, dysfunctional family while living in a middle-class neighbourhood, I felt unhappy, ashamed and riddled with feelings of inferiority. The lazy CEO in my head was at work contrasting my life in the context of the middle-class white kids I lived among. They seemed flawless and happy, so my comparison-seeking mind concluded that I was inferior and that I was not enough.

This damming conclusion of myself presented one clear answer: if I could just get the things that my lazy CEO mind used as a measure of comparison to conclude that I was inferior – if I could have the nice things, the perfect family, a perfect house and lots of money – I would finally be enough. So off I went, charging into the world in pursuit of everything I thought I needed, believing that it would fix something that was never broken and was only inferior in the irrational, toxic context that my lazy CEO comparison-obsessed brain had created.

What I didn't tell you was I was actually born in a small poor village in Botswana, in the south of Africa, where there was an average life expectancy of just 49 years at the turn of the century.

Had I not left that context as a baby, my family would have lived at the very top of the social ladder and I would likely have grown up feeling completely differently . . .

This is what happens when you bring together our abundant Western society, social media and our comparison-driven minds – people get miserable easily, mental health issues surge and suicide rates among young people climb.

The only worthwhile comparison is YOU yesterday vs YOU today. If you want to be happy, you have to focus on that.

Chapter Four

STOP KEEPING UP WITH THE KARDASHIANS

SO, HOW DO you beat that lazy CEO in your head?

The truth is that you can't.

You won't stop comparing yourself to others regardless of what I say because you won't stop being human. As tempting as it is for me to come up with some nonsense formula to end all negative comparisons, I can't bring myself to lie to you.

However – and this is a huge however – there are significant practical and scientifically proven actions you can choose to circumnavigate and take advantage of the way your mind works . . .

You will have heard of Kylie Jenner. She was reportedly a billionaire by the age of 21. She has flawless looks and a beautiful wealthy family, and she broadcasts her seemingly perfect, selectively filtered life several times a day to more than 300 million predominantly young girls who have made the conscious decision to follow her every move. One of her recent posts showed her 'perfect' toned, brown body leaning off a yacht floating through what I can only describe as paradise, wearing a designer bikini while sipping expensive champagne.

For a second, imagine a different young woman called 'Jenner Kylie'. Her name is the opposite way round and so is her life.

She's 21 years old and she lives hand to mouth in government housing, working two minimum-wage jobs to make ends meet. She has a natural curvaceous body shape, acne, cellulite and frizzy hair. Like most people her age, she spends between four and 10 hours a day on her phone.

Can you even imagine what she feels about herself subconsciously when her lazy CEO brain inevitably contrasts her life to that of Kylie Jenner? In that context, how could she ever feel that she's enough? The sad truth is that 'Jenner Kylie' won't realise why she's so anxious, insecure and self-conscious, and why she struggles with bouts of depression. She'll say that she loves watching Kylie Jenner because it's 'fun', 'entertaining' or 'inspiring' without realising the destructive mental cost of that 'entertainment'. Her decision to follow Kylie Jenner, and hundreds of seemingly perfect fake influencers like her, is an act of mental self-harm – maybe the greatest modern act of self-harm millennials unknowingly perpetrate on themselves.

FAKE IT TO MAKE IT

Dr Tijion Esho, the renowned cosmetic surgeon whose industry is booming in the social media era, admits that over one-third of his clients come to him with visual references of social media influencers that they want to look like when they request surgery, i.e. they bring a screenshot of a fake, filtered person and ask him to make them as unrealistic so they can show their followers and continue the cycle of toxic comparisons. Zeev Farbman, the CEO of Facetune, the app hundreds of millions of young people use to modify how their photos look – think of it as digital plastic surgery – says the app has been so popular that he feels like he's 'won the lottery'.

They say a picture paints a thousand words, so it's no surprise that Instagram, the platform designed for self-broadcasting your filtered life in pictures, was voted the worst social media platform for mental health and well-being according to a survey of 1,479 young people. It's even less surprising that Kylie Jenner too – at the heart of the issue – is not only part of the problem, she's a victim of it in equal measure. In a recent post she confessed that she has suffered with mental health issues for her 'whole young adult life'. After all, she now has to compete with the fake self-construct and the false superficial context she's built around herself – she has to run out of shops covering her face and wearing overly baggy clothes to avoid the devastating risk that the world's press might hold her to the unrealistic standard she's created for herself with the snap of one candid unedited, unfiltered and – god forbid – real photo.

At just 18 years old, Kylie had the word 'sanity' tattooed onto her hip because, in her words, 'I felt a little bit like I was going insane. Or, I was going to.'

I have nothing against Kylie. If anything I'm sympathetic to the environment she was born into – that wasn't her choice. But to the 300,000,000+ people following her, you do have a choice. The fact that you, and billions of others like you, are actively choosing to expose your lazy CEO, comparison-oriented minds to such a filtered, unrealistic and toxic environment every single day, for hours at a time, is a choice that you and the connected generation must reconsider if you are to get out alive. This is voluntary mental self-harm on an enormous scale. You wouldn't continue to read books that told you you're a worthless, ugly, unsuccessful piece of shit, so why have you chosen to fill a digital library with content that will evidently do the same?

Your lazy CEO mind, although lazy, is incredibly persistent and unbelievably dedicated to the cause of comparison. Despite how the self-help gurus might tell you to 'stop comparing yourself to other people', this is not useful advice – it's just a bunch of unhelpful words, words that don't appreciate the intrinsic nature of the human condition.

16-year-old me looked 'up' to 16-year-old Justin Bieber, and many of us look 'up' to celebrities, a more successful friend or a more fortunate colleague, determining that he or she is better than we are. 'They are so much happier and more successful than me' is an example of upward social comparison, like my hypothetical Jenner Kylie looking 'up' to Kylie Jenner. These types of upward comparison are uninformed and unfair. The truth is we come with our own personal advantages and disadvantages, strengths and weaknesses. In fact, there is nobody on planet Earth with the same biological make-up, life experience or social advantages or disadvantages as you. You are by any logical definition unique, so any comparison is inherently and logically unfair. According to an in-depth research paper by Carmen Carmona and her colleagues at the Department of Social and Organizational Psychology, our upward social comparisons typically foster feelings of helplessness, jealousy and inferiority, which will jeopardise our sense of identity and create an increased risk of feeling burnt out. Not a good idea.

'I am so much happier and more successful than they are' is an example of a downward social comparison; you look 'down' on someone that you believe is in a worse social position than you and determine that you or your situation is better than theirs. Again, it's not an inherently fair exercise as the individuals you look down on have their own unique biological dispositions, life experiences and social advantages and disadvantages, but we all occasionally compare ourselves with those who are worse off or less capable than ourselves in an effort to boost our own feelings of well-being and self-esteem. The science shows that this can work but only temporarily.

Our timelines have become our libraries and they're now one of the greatest influences over how we think and feel.

Unfollow fake, negative and uninspiring influencers, and follow honest, real and positive creators.

Upgrade your library.

Like my first Nokia brick phone glancing across the decades at my new iPhone 999, despite how 'entertaining' it might be to observe someone's manufactured superiority in the short-term, an unavoidable consequence of doing so in the long term is an increased chance of misery, 'compare and despair' syndrome, and an inferiority complex so crippling it might tempt you to create and then project on to others the same false flawlessness that caused you to feel so inadequate in the first place. Unfollow, block and mute – and not just online. Block these people in real life. Stop watching them on reality TV shows and (I'm aiming this part predominantly at men) stop gawking after other guys with their Lamborghinis and Instagram models. Ignore the hustle-porn gurus that sell you their get-rich-quick schemes on the same basis that Kylie sells hundreds of millions of dollars of cosmetics – i.e. that you are naturally inadequate. Make your context smaller, healthier and more real. I mean this when I say it – it might just save your life.

Social media has made 'perfect' look normal, so now 'good' has become disposable.

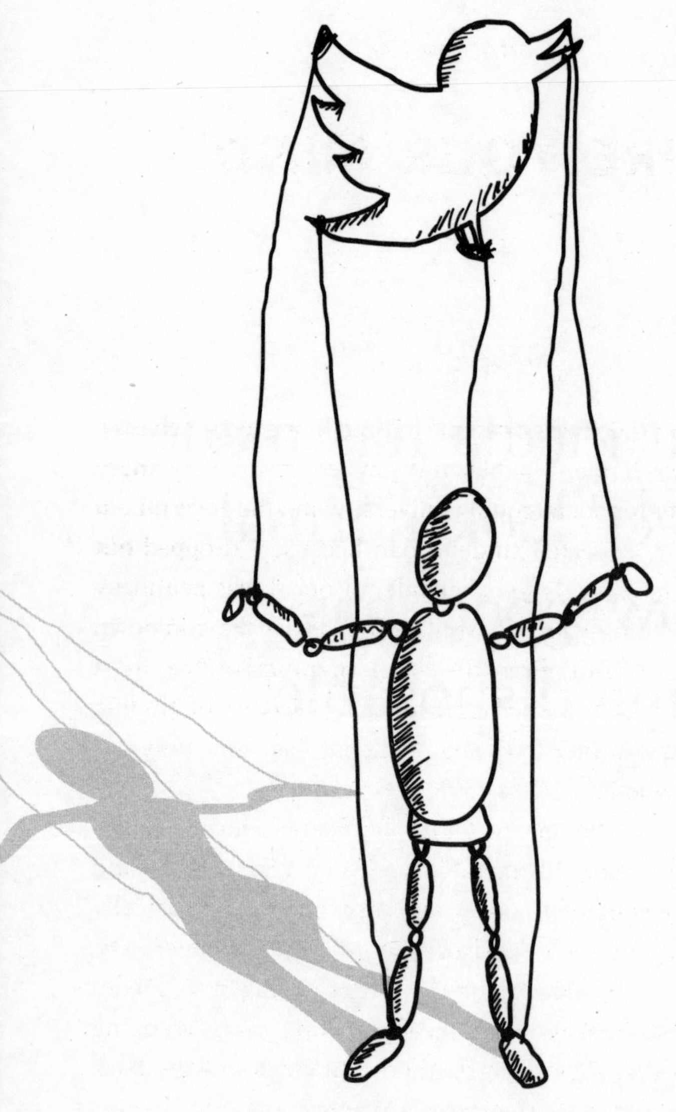

WE BECOME WHAT THE ALGORITHM
WANTS US TO BE.

Chapter Five

FIRE YOUR MIND

AT 18 YEARS OLD, I was unemployed and living in Manchester, 300 miles from home. I had been disowned by my very angry African mother for not attending university, and the government hadn't paid my expected student loan because I dropped out of university too quickly to be eligible for one. I was penniless, alone and so hungry that I would often leave the run-down house I shared with three illegal immigrants in the most dangerous part of the city with the sole objective of finding food, or money to buy food, that someone had hopefully left behind somewhere.

On some days this meant taking half-eaten chicken bones in takeaways or shoplifting Chicago Town pizzas if I could muster up the courage to do so, and on other days it basically meant relying on some kind of luck or random generosity. One day I was particularly lucky. After losing a 20p coin down the back of a seat in the takeaway shop I was scavenging in, I realised that they never bothered to clean out the back of their seats and, over the years, a profuse amount of coins had rolled down there and never been recovered. When I reached down to recover my coin, my hand returned filthy and clasping a £1 coin. Motivated by hope and hunger, I slowly moved around every table in their establishment, inconspicuously reaching down the back of their seats as I went and, to my surprise and delight, I recovered a total of £13.40 in loose change.

I cannot begin to describe to you how happy I felt that day. I left that takeaway with the biggest smile on my face and a spring in my step. Finding this money meant I could eat for the next few days, and not just eat. In relative terms I could eat well – bread, Pot Noodles, Marmite and all of my favourites.

Fast forward a few years, and I'm in a 5-star hotel room eating a gourmet breakfast when I receive the news that the company I founded at 21 years old has just been listed on the stock market with a valuation of roughly $200,000,000. This news multiplies my net worth into the eight-figure region, instantaneously making me one of the richest under-30s in the United Kingdom in that moment.

And I felt absolutely . . . Nothing.

Nada.

Completely indifferent.

I was shocked and worried that I felt so emotionless. I always imagined this moment would feel different – I imagined confetti, cheering, exhilaration. But what I got was nothing. I had genuinely felt happier when I found that £13 and 40 pence down the back of the filthy takeaway chairs than I did upon hearing that my company had been listed with a $200m valuation.

*

If a person could do only *one* simple thing to increase their health and happiness then expressing gratitude on a regular basis must be it.

Why the fuck didn't I just automatically feel happy and grateful? I called my business partner, Dominic, in the hope that his excitement would be somewhat contagious and to my horror he was in exactly the same mental state – he felt this total sense of anti-climax and numbness.

Confused, I decided I would put on my headphones and uncharacteristically walk to work that day. Ten minutes into my walk, a ripple of goosebumps surged across the skin of every part of my body like an unanticipated Mexican wave. The song 'Money Trees' by Kendrick Lamar had started in my headphones, a song that I had listened to every single day without fail when the 19-year-old me made the two-hour walk from a dilapidated, rodent-infested room above a Chinese takeaway I was living in to the call centre I worked night shifts at on the other side of town.

That song, like a musical time machine, teleported me back to my darkest days, the time when I dreamed of days like today; when I worked all night in call centres to get enough money to cover my rent and then all day on my business to try to get me out of the dire situation I was in. I walked to that call centre on these same streets, gawking at every apartment block I passed telling myself that one day I would have my own apartment, and at every car showroom I passed fantasising that one day I would be able to afford driving lessons and a car of my own.

Before the song had ended, tears were flooding down my face, and I felt an overwhelming sense of euphoria from the sense of gratitude that had engulfed me. Frantically, I pulled out my phone and sent my business partner a voice message taking him back to our darkest moments together, the early days of building the business when we slept on the same kitchen floors and sofas together and the moments when the business was hours away from bankruptcy. I talked him through the impact today would have on our team, our families and everyone that we loved the most. This exercise drastically changed his mood and within minutes the anaesthetised guy I had just spoken to was grateful, fired up, and happy too.

This was the moment that I truly realised the power of gratitude. Gratitude isn't an approach centred on removing your lazy CEO from office – as I said that isn't possible – it's one that focuses on giving your CEO additional healthier responsibilities – better context – that will help you to create a more positive self-assessment of how 'complete' you are.

From all the research I've studied on the topic of happiness, if a person could do only one simple mental exercise to increase their health and happiness then expressing gratitude on a regular basis is it.

Martin Seligman, a pioneer in the field of positive psychology (the study of the positive aspects of the human experience such as happiness and well-being), says that 'when we take time to notice the things that go right – it means we're getting a lot of little rewards throughout the day'. And that just feels like a bunch of fluffy words – until you look at the science. It's been proven that you can reward your mind by actively expressing gratitude. Every time a person expresses or receives gratitude, a chemical called dopamine – the 'feel-good' neurotransmitter releases in the brain.

To most people, this is not a huge surprise. Most of us realise that at the times when we feel most grateful for the circumstances of our lives, we feel most happy. So why do we practice gratitude so rarely? Why don't we do it all of the time?

We naturally live in constant forward motion, with lists of incomplete ambitions and our focus transfixed on tomorrow. As I said, we don't feel like we're ever enough, we struggle to feel truly accomplished despite our achievements and so how would we feel gratitude naturally?

That morning on my way to work, after achieving the biggest accomplishment of my life, I realised that we can't live life expecting gratitude to just show up on its own because it rarely ever does – we live with our heads so far in the future that it often doesn't have the chance to. We have to invite gratitude into our lives and we have to do it consciously and consistently.

The multi-million-pound windfall I had received that day had no automatic impact on me because the lazy CEO in my mind had already been at work weeks and months before that moment with it's unhealthy upward social comparisons, contrasting me to even more successful people, and in that context, I wasn't really that successful and today didn't really matter. In fact, every upward step I had taken in my career in the previous five years brought with it a new set of upwards comparisons that left me feeling like I was always not quite 'there', as if I had never really achieved something worth celebrating. This again is an unavoidable part of the human mind that has been immensely exacerbated by the advent of the internet and social media. Social media has given all of us an endless and unrealistic context in which to compare ourselves to others, and although we can't easily change our prehistoric wiring, we can subdue its power over us by being more consciously aware of what's happening, what's causing it and the impact it has on us.

A BILLIONAIRE'S DILEMMA

Research regularly points to two central questions that people ask themselves when determining whether they're satisfied with something in their life:

- Am I doing better than I was before? (A historic self-comparison.)
- Am I doing better than other people? (An upward or downward social comparison.)

This applies to wealth, but also to attractiveness, height and other things that the society and social circle you live in value.

But a lot of the things that really matter in our lives we find hard to measure. If you wanted to be a good parent/partner/boss, it's hard for your brain to decide if you're a better parent/partner/boss now than you were a year ago, and it's also hard to know if you're a better parent/partner/boss than your neighbours or friends. For the easy – life-seeking, rapid – comparison-reliant lazy CEO in your brain that's simply too much work.

That's when people turn to dimensions of comparison that can be easily quantified, and in today's world that is followers on Instagram, money, industry awards, job titles, the square footage of your house, a verification checkmark on your social media profile, the cost of your clothes and other quantifiable social and/or material metrics. But here's the thing – troves of research show that this predisposition to measure and compare has no end; it doesn't disappear once people have a ridiculous amount of money, cars, houses or status. If you win the lottery tomorrow and upgrade to a new neighbourhood like most people would, you'll quickly realise that you're still a lot less rich than some of the people within your new life, hence the ever-shifting goalposts at all levels of wealth and the ever-changing level of satisfaction.

The feeling of being rich is not about fulfilling some childhood dream, of buying the Range Rover that 18-year-old me dreamed about; feeling wealthy is largely just about comparison with others in your reference group. And my reference group on that day of the stock market announcement had drastically changed. At 12 years old, all I needed was the new Nokia brick phone to rank at the top of my secondary school reference group, but a billionaire needs an extra 50ft on their super-yacht to achieve the same sense of adequacy.

Harvard Business School Professor Michael Norton studied the connections between happiness and wealth and asked over 2,000 people with a net worth of at least $1 million (including many whose wealth far exceeded that threshold) how happy they were on a scale of 1 to 10, and then he asked them how much more money they would need to get to a 10. He said that all the way up the income wealth spectrum, everyone says they'd just need two or three times as much money as they have now' to be perfectly happy. That is – people with £1m think they'd need £2m to £3m to be perfectly happy, and those with £10m think they'd just need £20m to £30m to be happy! I'm sorry, but isn't that nuts?

This starkly illustrates an essential, yet unappreciated, truth: that if you go through life believing that happiness is somewhere in your future, it always will be – it will never be where you are now. We're increasingly sold the idea that perfect happiness is hiding behind one more promotion, one more pay cheque or one thousand more followers. And we're sold this lie by the marketing industry (my industry – by people like me), by those who have achieved what we're seeking and are feigning perfect happiness online as part of a wider status game, and by that lazy CEO brain that is incapable of the hard work required to value things for what they really are.

'A THEORY OF HUMAN MOTIVATION'

Another way to understand why I was apathetic on a day which many would expect to be the best day of my life can be understood through the framework of Maslow's famous hierarchy of needs. It's the widely recognised motivational theory in psychology – a five-tier model of human needs, often depicted within a pyramid.

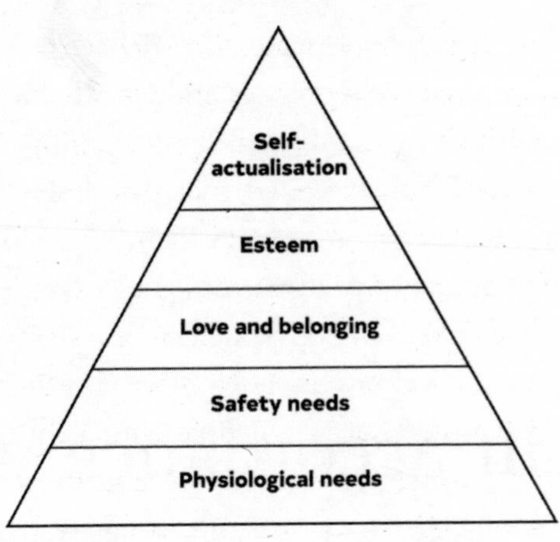

Maslow's Hierarchy of Needs

Maslow stated that our most basic need is for physical survival, and that this will be the first thing that motivates our behaviour. That £13.40 I dug out from the back of the grotty seats at 18 years old helped me to meet a burning need for survival that day – it met my physiological needs so it's no surprise that it felt so disproportionately rewarding. Maslow specified that once a certain level of the pyramid is fulfilled, the next level up is what motivates us, and so on and so on – he asserted that once complete, the previous level would not deliver the same degree of motivation as it had previously.

By 26 years old, I was already financially free enough to provide for my material needs, so going from being financially free on a large six-figure salary to tens of millions quite frankly did nothing for me. If you had told me this when I was broke, I wouldn't have a) believed you, and b) if I did, I still would have pursued it anyway. As a young, broke guy, I knew the popular clichéd phrase 'money doesn't buy you happiness' but the voice in my head would reply with something like 'Oh, shut the fuck up. I'll definitely be happier when I get that Lamborghini.'

Live in accordance with your outside world and you'll soon find misery.

Live in accordance with your inside world and you'll soon find happiness.

A study published in 2018 by researchers at Purdue University found that once we reach a certain household income of about £72,500/$95,000 globally, more income tended to be associated with equal or reduced life satisfaction and a lower level of well-being, i.e. more and more money, once your core needs are met, won't have an impact on your life satisfaction at all.

I was wrong, it's as simple as that. Money does matter – having the financial freedom to buy what I need, live in a comfortable, heated home and be able to travel is great. Beyond that, though, it is nothingness, and judging by the impression that my closest billionaire friends have given me privately, maybe even misery. Of all the lessons I learned in the process of going from totally broke to rich, this is the lesson I am most deeply thankful I learned now – before I spent copious amounts of time, money and energy on material things in a wild goose chase for pleasure and status, mistaking it for happiness.

A NEW HEALTHY HABIT

As I approached my office that day and the tears of gratitude began to dry on my face, I made a pledge to myself that I would no longer just expect gratitude to show up in my life and, although I knew I couldn't fire my lazy CEO in my mind, I could give him a set of healthier daily responsibilities by assigning him the task of performing frequent downward self-comparisons. Put simply, I would frequently stop and take the time to remind myself of how far I have come, and how amazing that is.

I decided that as often as I can, the last thing I would do before I fall asleep, and the first thing I would do in the morning, is write one thing in the notes section of my phone that I'm grateful for – sometimes these are just words such as 'my niece' or 'Pablo' (my dog) and sometimes they are essays. Sometimes

I don't write them down, sometimes I use music to take me back in time or photos to remind me of key moments. I'm not into airy-fairy personal development bullshit – I promise you, I'm one of the most naturally sceptical, logic-seeking people you're likely to meet – but this little gratitude exercise has transformed the way I see my world. It's made everything and everyone in my life a little bit sweeter and better appreciated.

It's made me more optimistic and it's made my romantic relationship feel even more special, worthwhile and meaningful.

I understood the neurological impact that gratitude had on dopamine levels but couldn't explain why such a small daily habit, something that cost me an average 20 seconds each day, was having such a momentous impact on my overall feeling of fulfilment so, in my characteristically curious way, I spent the best part of six months trawling through all of the available research on the matter and what I found was astounding.

One study conducted by Lan Chaplin that I read about in the *Journal of Positive Psychology* showed that keeping a gratitude journal decreased materialism and the desire to have more stuff and also resulted in a 60 per cent increase in charitable donations. This makes a tremendous amount of sense when you consider what we saw during the 2020 global coronavirus pandemic. Our timelines became full of death, fear and suffering. Not only did this make us fasten our purse strings, and deny us of an opportunity to show off our material possessions, but it also forced many of us into an involuntary downward social comparison – we became more grateful than ever before for our families, for our health and for our lives, and sales of designer goods plummeted. According to one report by ThredUp – the world's largest online store for luxury second hand clothes – 50% more people decided to sell their luxury goods post-Covid than they did pre-Covid.

THE GRASS WILL ALWAYS LOOK GREENER ON THE OTHER SIDE.

UNTIL YOU START WATERING THE SIDE YOU'RE ON.

Causality is hard to determine here because of the economic and social impacts of the pandemic, but I have a strong belief that an increase in gratitude decreased materialism during the pandemic. My business partner Dom is a prime example of this – he's a guy that I've never seen without his beautiful gold Rolex, but surprisingly he hasn't worn it once since the pandemic began.

All of this, and the evidence that I've shared in previous chapters suggests that we seemingly don't feel such a strong compulsion to buy Louis Vuitton bags and Rolex watches if we have strong feelings of gratitude. After all, the force that makes you want to spend thousands of pounds to own these designer goods relies on you feeling like you're not enough in the first place. Maybe I wouldn't have felt so much inadequacy and the need to become a sexy millionaire if I was able to be a little more grateful when I was younger. Those powerful, adolescent, unhealthy upward comparisons made it seemingly impossible for me to be grateful. Maybe my career success is a direct result of my lack of gratitude and the deep feelings of inadequacy it gave me. Maybe if I had never realised this, I would just be another miserable millionaire chasing after material possessions mistaking it for happiness.

Other studies on the topic of gratitude have shown how gratitude journals lead to healthier eating behaviours and fewer negative emotions. Cumulatively the research agrees that contributing to a gratitude journal at any frequency between once a day to once a week had substantial positive effects on well-being.

In many respects, my gratitude journal has become my fight-back against my own lazy CEO mind and the toxic society it functions in. Gratitude has transformed me from feeling that what I have isn't enough, to feeling like it's more than enough – and it's made me feel like I'm enough.

Actively practising gratitude feels so necessary in the modern era because our brains weren't designed to deal with all this social noise or the algorithms that feed me the prettiest, richest, smartest people on earth every day. Psychologists have often suggested that the slow pace of human evolution and the leap of cultural and technological change have meant that our minds are better adapted to our hunter-gatherer past (where 95 per cent of human evolution took place) than to today's supposedly fast-changing world. In short, digital technology has the capacity to overwhelm our prehistoric brains by exploiting their biases, vulnerabilities and limitations in subconscious, invisible ways. We don't see it happening, but the astronomical growth of anxiety and other mental health issues in the modern era suggests we're feeling the consequences.

Instead of dragging yourself out of bed today, hating life, and pulling that bad attitude through the week with you, try reminding yourself of how grateful you are to have work and how lucky you are to be alive.

Life has a funny way of giving grateful people even more things to be grateful for.

RELIGIOUSLY GRATEFUL

That sense of inherent gratitude and feeling beholden to the sacrifices and contributions of those who put you here is something the religious community knows well – it's the central component of religious worship. Christians express their gratitude for the sacrifices of Jesus in every song, in every prayer and at every Sunday service. Muslims live in gratitude to Allah. There is no worship without gratitude, and religion is worship.

So with that, you would understandably expect religious people around the world to be notably happier than non-religious, and you would be absolutely right. Every reputable study on the topic that has compared the lives of religious and non-religious people from over two dozen countries has shown that religious people live happier lives.

Actively religious people tend to be happier

% who say they are *'very happy'*, among those who are religious...

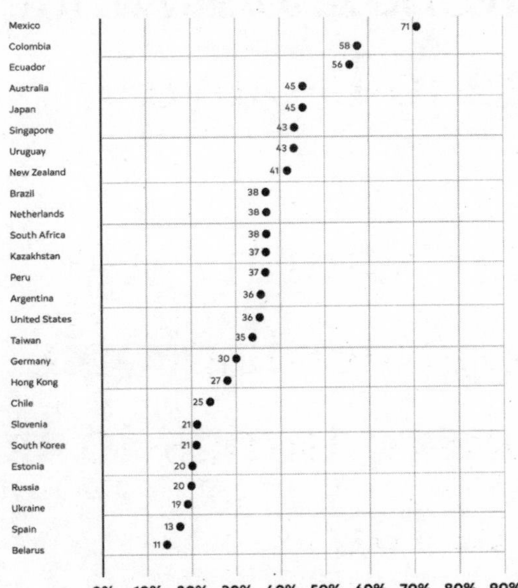

NOTE: The actively religious are those who identify with a religion and attend religious services at least once per month. Data sourced from PEW Research Center.

Gratitude has transformed me from feeling that what I have isn't enough, to feeling like it's more than enough – and it's made me feel like *I'm* enough.

In fact, clergy rank #1 in terms of fulfilment at work, and after evaluating thousands of points of research, the National Institute of Health reported that the incidence of suicide is notably less among religious than non-religious people.

Of course, religion is a complex and multifaceted experience so establishing reliable causality between a religious sect who are less likely to smoke or drink and more likely to talk about their problems and enjoy a sense of community – all factors conducive to positive well-being and mental health – isn't so straightforward.

But if the science on gratitude is to be trusted, then there can be no doubt that their perpetual and eternal sense of gratitude is an overwhelmingly positive contributor to the superior levels of happiness they enjoy.

I'm the atheist son of two devout Christian parents, and I was born into a world of relative comfort where most of my peers worship nothing more than Instagram influencers, reality show stars, successful athletes and material things – so it's no surprise that genuine gratitude doesn't come naturally to me.

I realise that I can't ever become the richest, prettiest or the smartest. I also realise that the drive to become any of those things is likely one fuelled by ungratefulness, and ungratefulness is the mother of unhappiness. So I know that I . . . we, the connected generation . . . must ardently reject the desire to embark on any such journey, and endeavour instead to focus the saved time and energy on being grateful now – an idea that's easier said than done.

The sheer fact that you're sat here reading this book shows just how much you have to be grateful for. What an absolute privilege it is for us to even be thinking about these existential things. My great-grandparents in Africa had to contend with poverty and the more than 10 hungry mouths that they struggled to feed. Their central concern was survival, and if you go back far enough in your family tree, I'm sure many of your ancestors suffered through similar circumstances. If you're a first- or second-generation immigrant from a developing country, it's likely that you won't have to go back that far. And here we all are – thanks to their love – warm, fed and sheltered, with the luxury to ponder our purpose, to search for fulfilment and to deliberate over meaning. What a remarkable privilege you have.

Be grateful, for gratitude can bring life to life, it can turn a meal to a feast, resentment to love, a grudge to forgiveness, an enemy to a friend, a disease to hope and you to enough.

Chapter Six

A HAPPY JUGGLER

I CAN'T THINK of many things that have done more damage to the mental peace of this connected generation than the socially propagated fairy tales about how our lives are *supposed* to be going. You're *supposed* to be married by now, you're *supposed* to have a mortgage, you're *supposed* to have kids, you're *supposed* to have a 'real' job, savings, a car, a plan, a passion and all of the answers, and you're *supposed* to be happy. This fairy tale of a *complete life* has been broadcast into the core of our self-perception for so long, with unrelenting consistency and with such a casual presumption, that it has somehow nonchalantly bypassed any reasonable conscious scrutiny and has become the accepted standard for all of our lives – regardless of circumstance. As I said earlier, how can we be sold anything without billboards, magazines, radio and social media first convincing us that there's something we don't have but so desperately need and/or that we are not enough?

Fairy tales will fuck up your life.

Life is certain chaos – it is the quest for continued forward motion in the pursuit of happiness. However, it appears that so many of us have misunderstood the purpose of this pursuit. On the day someone offered me millions to buy my company when I was just 24 years old, I abruptly realised that I had misunderstood the purpose of all of this too. Remember that life is not a finite game.

We think that when we are striving for something – which is most of the time – we're doing so in a state of chaos and dissatisfaction and that if we were only to accomplish our goal, we would gain the order and satisfaction that we are seeking. But that's not how it really works. The truth that I've unmistakably witnessed in my own life is that achieving all of our goals is what ultimately leads to chaos and dissatisfaction – whereas the state of striving actually provides us with stability and satisfaction.

An accomplished goal brings with it a loss of orientation and the risk of being swayed towards the chaos of purposelessness and psychological destabilisation. There is often discomfort in the act of striving for something – such as hard work, failure, rejection and fatigue – and we confuse this for chaos, but it's ironically the act of striving that keeps us stable. Paradoxically, our chaos is our order, and the happiness we're pursuing is the pursuit of happiness itself. So even if it were possible to have everything at once – if the fairy tale wasn't a fairy tale – it would be a thoroughly unfulfilling life to live.

If you were growing up in Greece some 2,500 years ago and your parents wanted you to get a decent education, rather than shipping you off to the nearest comprehensive school, they would have sent you to become well-versed in the study of philosophy. If you were especially fortunate, you may have been able to learn with the Stoics, a school of philosophy which is still incredibly well known today. Among other things, the Stoics taught something called 'τη φιλοσοφία της ζωής'.

The fairy tales of how life is 'supposed to be going' will fuck up your life. You don't have to go to university at 18, get a job at 21, buy a house at 30, get married at 35 and have kids at 36. Everyone is completely different and your path to happiness will be completely different too.

Don't worry, I also don't know how to even start to pronounce those words, but in English it means 'the philosophy of life'. The Stoics considered two things in life worth pursuing: 'virtue' (how we live happy lives) and 'tranquillity' (a lucid state characterised by ongoing freedom from distress).

The Stoics knew that one of the innate components of the human condition was insatiable consumerism; they observed how humans always seem to want more, and then even more once they had more. This is a phenomenon that psychologists call the 'hedonic treadmill' – where you lust after a new possession such as a new car or a flashy handbag, then you attain it, enjoy it for a short while, but soon your new item loses its joy. Eventually, you start to take it for granted and off you go in the pursuit of something new and better. You have to keep walking to stay in the same place.

This phenomenon was so blatant to the Stoics that they devised two ways to overcome it.

The first was 'negative visualisation'. For an idea of how negative visualisation works, imagine that the things and people you take for granted, like family or close friends, suddenly vanish. The feeling of loss is awful.

This is ultimately a 2,500 year old gratitude exercise, like my aforementioned gratitude diary, or that song that played during my walk to work on the day my company was listed on the stock market. It's an exercise that gives you a chance to contemplate how lucky you are to still have them around you in reality. The Stoics asserted that learning to appreciate what you have would allow you to enjoy the world in a much more profound way.

The second solution saw negative visualisation taken one step further to something called 'voluntary discomfort'. This practice is based on what the famous Roman Stoic philosopher Seneca called 'to practise poverty'.

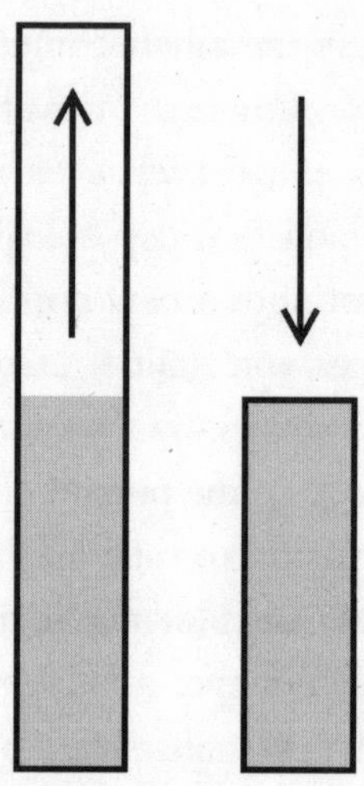

"THE SECRET OF HAPPINESS, YOU SEE, IS NOT FOUND IN SEEKING MORE, BUT IN DEVELOPING THE CAPACITY TO ENJOY LESS."

SOCRATES

Simply put, this means abstaining from something so that you can truly appreciate the value of it when you gain access to it again. The Stoics believed in one simple truth that was perfectly articulated by the Ancient Greek philosopher Socrates: 'The secret of happiness, you see, is not found in seeking more, but in developing the capacity to enjoy less.' That not having everything you want is part of what makes what you do have so special.

I CHOOSE WAFFLES

I love waffles. Maybe more than any human that has ever lived. I love Nutella on top, caramel sauce, crushed Oreos, ice cream, you name it – put it all on the top! If I could, I would undoubtedly have five waffles a day, maybe more. However, I also really love having abs. The whole world gawks at someone with great abs because the social value of having a six-pack is pretty remarkable. But have you ever really considered why? You might say 'because it's sexy'. But that's just another adjective. Why is it sexy? The answer, as it is with all 'things' in life, is because of the story attached to it.

Abs take tremendous discipline, strength and hard work. Outside of an evolutionary survival perspective, abs mean you are disciplined, active and that you don't eat five waffles a day! If it was possible to eat five waffles every day and have abs, they would just be lines on our stomach and they would have no perceived social 'value'. (One might also predict that if I did have five waffles every day, the waffles too would lose their sense of specialness.)

These two desires – five waffles a day and a six-pack – cannot co-exist. They're mutually exclusive, and that's ultimately what makes each feel special to me in their own right. Therefore, part of the value of anything lives not in the thing, but in the story of all of the things you said no to in order to have it. And you can extrapolate this principle to every area of your life – choosing not to go after every hot person you meet is part of what makes your commitment to one partner so valuable. Maybe this is the value of life, maybe self-restraint is the thing that makes things feel so precious, but in an increasingly unsatisfied and consumerist world that's driven by persuading you there's something you don't have but so desperately need, and one supported by a technological infrastructure that has made it appear easier now than at any time in human history to get it (Amazon Prime, Tinder, online get-rich-quick schemes), it would seem that this idea is something that's been substituted with a disturbing culture of modern gluttony.

In 2017, if you look at the numbers (adjusted for inflation), Americans (living in arguably the home of Western consumerism) spent twice as much as in 2002 on goods like jewellery, watches, books, luggage and telephones, according to the Bureau of Economic Analysis. Spending on personal care products also doubled over that time period. Americans spent, on average, 20 per cent more money on clothes than in 2000. The average American bought 7.4 pairs of shoes, up from 6.6 pairs in 2000 (although, on average, humans maintained the same number of feet throughout that period).

With these increasing mountains of largely meaningless stuff, of course, people now need even bigger houses in which to hoard them. Predictably, the Harvard Joint Center for Housing Studies showed a 23 per cent increase in home size from just two decades ago, and an equally foreseeable collection of research shows cheating on partners has steadily increased among millennials.

Juggling is part of our history. There are Egyptian paintings of people juggling balls that date back as much as 4,000 years.

Juggling relies on a variety of limiting factors: hand speed, accuracy, aerial space and the size of the human hand (you need to be able to grasp X number of balls). On top of this, the more balls you juggle, the higher you've got to throw them to create the space needed to avoid mid-air collisions – which requires even more accuracy, speed and, ideally, an even larger hand. Because of these limiting factors, physicists estimate that it's almost impossible for an adult human to juggle more than 14 balls – the current undisputed world record. Anyone that has tried to juggle more than 14 balls has always failed.

To me, this has always been a beautiful metaphor for life. There is a fundamental limit to how many balls you're able to juggle. So you have to choose which balls you want to juggle and which are the most meaningful to hold. The foolish endeavour to juggle them all will only result in failure. And the balls you do choose to juggle will feel significantly more valuable, because they were chosen at the expense of all of the other balls that you simply couldn't hold.

I guess what I'm trying to say is, I choose waffles.

Chapter Seven

WE'RE ALL BEING FUCKED BY BINARY BOXES

WHAT'S YOUR PASSION? Have you found your purpose? Is it love? What's your why? Are they your soulmate?

I'm so sick of people asking me these stupid fucking questions.

Welcome to the world of toxic, loaded, presumptive, invalid, naive questions that our modern society can't seem to live without. These questions and ones like them are broadcast through TED talks, social media influencers, self-development books and self-help experts. And by 'successful' people like me with large followings who can't appreciate the fact that their circumstances are fundamentally unique, that everyone is fundamentally different, and that, in many respects, they were incredibly lucky to stumble into something that provides them with the key ingredients of a successful, rewarding life.

These toxic questions, words and statements are the cause of disproportionate amounts of anxiety, stress and chronic overthinking in today's society. I call bullshit on all of them.

What if I asked you: 'What colour is four?' or 'What number is orange?'. . . Exactly.

‘Follow your passion’ has become a powerful piece of anxiety-inducing career bullshit.

Just because you can ask a question doesn't make it inherently valid. I want to put all of these questions in the bin. Ban them.

Fuck free speech, if I ever get to become the prime minister, all these phrases are going to be illegal. Any use of any of them and you're getting life behind bars.

BULLSHIT ADVICE AND WHERE IT CAME FROM

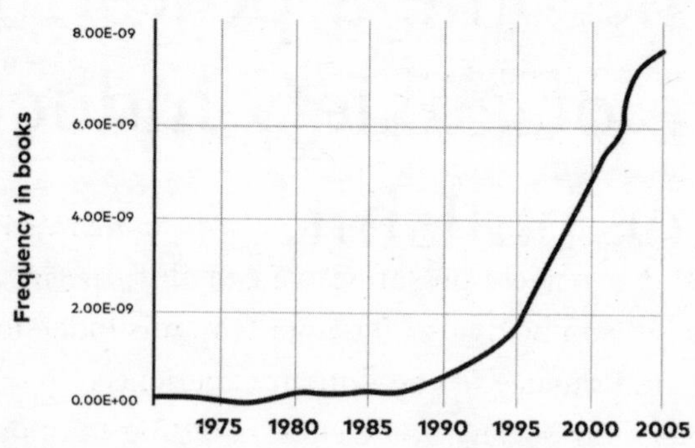

I don't really know where to start. I don't get angry easily but, as you can tell, as I write this chapter I feel a cauldron of warmth bubbling inside me. I think it's because I've seen first-hand the damage that these invalid questions have done to people, to relationships, to careers, to my younger employees and to the collective mental well-being of a very easily influenced generation. I receive thousands and thousands of messages each year from people of all ages who are worried because they don't know their 'why', haven't 'found their passion' or can't figure out if they're 'in love' with their 'soulmate' or not. These seemingly innocent words, questions and statements, that were well-intended to provide direction, have actually had the adverse effect and caused more people to feel lost than ever before. These loaded questions have the remarkable ability to make a perfectly happy person question if they actually are. And because society makes everything look perfect and binary, imperfect and complex feel wrong. Life is imperfect and complex, but life isn't wrong.

We are incredibly multifaceted, uniquely complex, ever-evolving beings. We're constructed from 7 billion atoms, 37 trillion cells and millions of intimate individual experiences, viewing the world through two unique eyes with one completely individual perspective.

We feel different things.

We see different things.

We think in different ways.

So any binary question seeking a yes or no answer like the ones above, that naively presumes we can all fit perfectly into the same yes or no box, has fundamentally misunderstood the complexity and nuance of the human experience.

As a developing society, we're slowly starting to understand that things aren't binary – and how wrong we've been. Too recently we've realised that sexuality and gender aren't binary – but before we did, the pressure we exerted on young people to fit into society's boxes caused untold depression, anxiety, self-loathing and suicide and, to be honest, it still does.

Research still shows that attempted suicide rates and suicidal ideation among the lesbian, gay, bisexual and transgender community are drastically higher than in the general population.

As history has shown, an attempt to force a complex human or nuanced issue into a simple binary box is one that will be filled with anxiety and discomfort for everybody involved.

Society makes everything look perfect and binary, so imperfect and complex feel wrong.

Life is imperfect and non-binary, but life isn't wrong.

Moreover, research studying the notion that humans have a fixed 'passion' has demonstrated that this perspective harms motivation for everything outside of the singular passion and that you're more likely to quit your 'passion' when times get tough than those with a more fluid view of their interests.

These words and phrases – 'your soulmate', 'your passion', 'your calling' – have been invented by a Western culture and they're loaded with toxic presumptions that: a) you have some pre-formed, pre-determined, fixed singular 'soulmate', 'passion' or 'why' that must be hunted down like a metaphorical Easter egg, and b) when you find this Easter egg, it'll feel the same for you as it does for the other 8 billion unique beings on earth – so much so that you'll be able to simply answer yes or no, and jump into a binary box when I ask you if you've found 'it' yet. I'm sorry, but this is a tragically large amount of bullshit. The truth is, people have multiple 'passions'; they're fluid and evolve with age, wisdom and experience. It would appear that my two-year-old niece's central 'passion' is to cover her eyes with her hands and then quickly remove them and shout 'peek-aboo' – I'm hoping she's not still pursuing that passion at 40.

"FINDING YOURSELF"
IS A POP CULTURE LIE.

"FINDING YOUR PASSION"
IS A POP CULTURE LIE.

"FINDING YOUR SOULMATE"
IS A POP CULTURE LIE.

THERE IS NOTHING TO FIND,
ONLY TO CREATE.

Chapter Eight

MUM, STOP ASKING ME ABOUT LOVE

THERE IS NO script for life.

Marriage isn't right for everyone, a 9–5 isn't best for everything, one job for the rest of your life or having kids or living in one place won't suit all. My ability to resist conforming to the script, to resist trying to squeeze into society's binary boxes or answer invalid questions and write fresh rules for how my life will be lived is unquestionably much of the reason I found success and happiness in the way I did.

It goes against conventional thinking, but with staggering rates of depression, marital breakdowns, burnout, anxiety and purposelessness, maybe we need some more unconventional thinking.

Speaking of binary boxes, every time I tell a close friend or family member that I have a girlfriend, they quickly greet this news with, 'Are you in love?' or, 'Is it love?'

In an instant, I feel my cognitive processes start to overheat, malfunction and slam into a brick wall of perplexity as I desperately search for an agreed-upon simple definition for one of the world's most complex, over-used and inherently subjective words: love.

There is no script for life.

'Hmm. What the fuck is a "love"?' my brain whispers back.

Finding one common explanation shared between all 8 billion inhabitants of Earth is an incredible challenge, especially when the word is used so often. People LOVE their dog, they LOVE Marmite, they LOVE their job. How can we agree upon the definition of the phrase 'in love' when no human can feel what any other human is feeling. Right?

The truth is, I will never know if what I feel towards my girlfriend is the same as your definition of that complicated word – certainly not adequately enough to offer you a yes or no answer to the question, 'Are you in love?' and I'm perfectly okay with that. I'm okay with the idea that my experience is an extremely individual, ever-evolving, somewhat indescribable one. I don't need to put additional needless social pressure on a good thing – I don't need to squeeze my individual experience into a binary societal box to know that my relationship with my girlfriend is meaningful and worthwhile, and I really don't know why it should matter to anyone else either.

They say 'birds of a feather flock together' and swans do exactly that. Like many other creatures in the animal kingdom, miraculously they manage to hold lifelong committed relationships without ever needing to 'put a ring on it', without ever asking each other if they're 'in love', and without any other swan's approval – they just seem to know, and they're okay with that. They accept the joint responsibility of taking care of each other. Both partners work on building the home and both partners share egg incubation duties. They enjoy each other for who they are, not who they wish they were. And they commit to raising a family together for life.

Maybe we should all be more like the swan.

How can we agree upon the definition of the phrase 'in love' when no human can feel what any other human is feeling?

———

TILL DEATH DO US PART

In preparation for this book I asked hundreds of married people to answer the question: 'what's the point in marriage?' Those in support of the concept usually defaulted to explaining how much they've managed to achieve in their marriage. When I asked them if they thought they would have been able to achieve that without the legal contract of marriage, in every instance – sometimes after a period of reflection – the person answered 'yes'.

I think this rebuttal helped me and them to distinguish between the legal contract of marriage and the concept of a loving, long-term, committed relationship – two very different things.

On a few occasions people cited the joy of their wedding day as a reason for their marriage – but, of course, you can still have a wedding celebration without marriage. You can have kids, commitment, love, rings and all the trappings without the marriage.

Believe it or not, I'm not actually anti-marriage, I'm anti-marriage-for-everyone. Marriage might be a good arrangement that increases happiness and improves the quality of their relationship for some. For others, it won't be. For me, I don't think it will be, not least because I don't believe the law or religion should have any say in the love I have for someone (their track record on love is abysmal). But also because I've been happiest in my romantic relationships when I don't cohabit, have more freedom and am less attached.

And this is really my point, 'love' is one of life's many bespoke, personal and unique experiences. How you foster your love and build your relationship should therefore be equally bespoke. I believe that it isn't the accomplishment of society's expectations that will make you happiest, it's the rejection of them. It's the ability to write a new set of rules for your life, based on what is true for you and based on the world you're living in now.

Our world is a much different place to how it was when most of these ideas and solutions were devised. We have the internet, more information, longer lives and more choices. If this isn't cause enough to at least try to re-imagine the outdated blueprint of how you're 'supposed' to live your life, of how you're 'supposed' to love, then I don't know what is.

It's ironic that these binary boxes, invalid questions and social blueprints were intended to protect and to guide us, but they seem to be doing the exact opposite – causing tremendous harm, making us feel lost and leading us to confusion and misery.

The hardest and most important thing you can do is to resist. If you truly care about being happy in your life and successful in your work, you have little choice. You have to become the author of your own 'script', one written by your heart, not one directed by your society.

Chapter Nine

CREATING YOUR PASSION

A GUY I met a few years ago recently admitted on national radio that he has a passion for building pretend double-decker buses using old wine crates, and painting little waving people on them – his name is Boris Johnson. He didn't manage to make a career of his passion, but it's worked out pretty well for him regardless.

Research shows that intrinsically motivating work makes people a lot happier than a big pay cheque. Part of the issue with the 'find your passion' narrative is that it implies that once you've found it, everything will follow: challenge, income, progress, success and fulfilment.

I reviewed over 60 different studies, published over the span of two decades, on the topic of finding your 'dream job' and it's clear that this is quite frankly bullshit.

Growing up, I was obsessive about playing football, writing hip-hop songs and building dens in the woods behind my house using whatever rubble I could find. As you can tell, I didn't make it as a building, rapping football player (there's still time), but I found complete job satisfaction in something entirely different – something I honestly never considered a 'passion' until I was in it.

The usual approach people take to work out their dream job is they imagine different jobs they know and ask themselves if they would enjoy those jobs. Or they reflect on jobs they've taken in the past and identify which bits they did and didn't like. At 17 years old, my career advisor in school told me to write out a list of things I wanted from work – like 'lots of money', 'to work with animals' and so on. The best-selling career advice book of all time, *What Color is Your Parachute?* by Richard N. Bolles, recommends exactly this. The hope is that, deep down, people already know what they really want, that they're destined for just one thing and in writing it down or verbalising it, the stars will somehow simply align. Bullshit. And toxic. Such toxic bullshit.

I'm sure you can think of many times in your life that you were excited to do something or to get something – a big night out, a date with a crush, new designer trainers, a trip or a new job – and it turned out to be underwhelming, disappointing and regrettable. This is incredibly common. Scientists have shown that we're actually really bad at forecasting what will make us happy, and we don't even realise how useless we are at this.

We're also terrible at remembering how satisfying different experiences were at the time. One confounding part of the human condition is that we tend to judge an experience primarily by its ending. For example, if you miss your flight at the start of a holiday, it will matter drastically less to your recollection of how enjoyable the holiday was, than if you miss your flight at the end of your holiday.

Unfortunately, we can't be trusted.

EASY MONEY!

Every time my mum sees me at Christmas time she inevitably, and with loving intent, tells me to make sure I'm getting paid properly and to avoid all stress. I'm sure you've heard the narrative that getting a higher salary will make you exponentially more happy and that stress is bad for you. In fact, the word stress only ever seems to be used in a negative context and within our culture it is intrinsically associated with mental health issues.

However, when you look at the modern literature on money and stress, the truth is more complex. Money, as I've already discussed, doesn't scale satisfaction after a certain point. And stress, as it relates to work, can be a good thing.

Those with jobs that we would all consider the most 'stressful' – such as military leaders, high-ranking government officials and CEOs – have been found to have lower levels of stress hormones and less anxiety despite poor sleeping patterns and huge responsibilities. One widely supported explanation is that these people have a greater sense of control (by setting their own working schedules, defining their own tasks and calling their own shots) and this protects them against the demands of the position.

Having demands that drastically exceed your abilities and level of competence is overwhelming and does cause harmful stress but having a very undemanding job can be deeply unrewarding too. The sweet spot is where the demands placed on you match your actual abilities and your self-perceived abilities – that makes for a fulfilling challenge.

SIMPLE SELLS, COMPLEX DOESN'T

'Find your passion' is extraordinarily bad advice. But it sells, because simple answers to complex problems always sell. If I wrote a book called *The One Simple Secret to Happiness,* I guarantee it would sell a lot better than a book called *The 10,000 Ingredients of Happiness.*

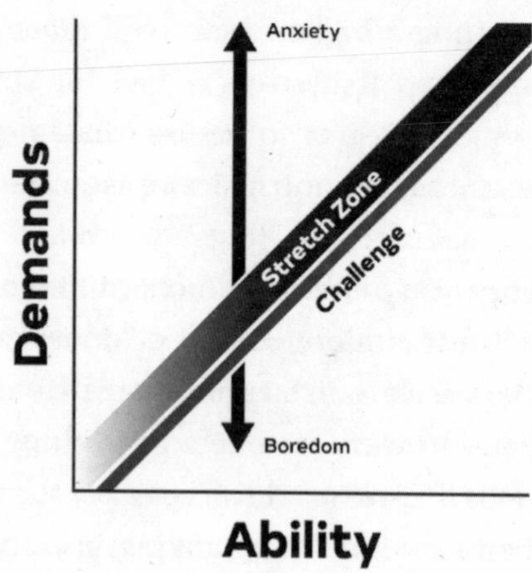

I was in Barcelona last year to deliver a talk about business and life to an audience of some 10,000 people. After the talk, a guy approached me and asked me the question: 'How did you become a great public speaker? Can you give me the top three secrets so that I can become one this year too.' And just like my close friends and family probing me to find out if I'm 'in love', in an instant I felt my cognitive processes start to overheat again. They malfunctioned and slammed into another brick wall of bewilderment as I desperately searched for a simple answer to a very complex question.

In essence, he was hoping I would give him three 'secret' short-cuts so that he could achieve the results born of more than a decade of hard work, failure, luck, timing, nature, nurture and persistence, with the hope that it would enable him to achieve, in a few short minutes, what it's taken me several years to master. Metaphorically, he saw me holding a very sharp sword, and he asked where he could buy one without knowing that you can't buy swords like this. You have to make them and, if you start now, in 10 years' time you might have one too.

Eurgh. . . That requires 'patience' and how can 'generation right now' wait for anything?

I genuinely believe that people who exercise patience and self-restraint over long periods of time, who work towards a worthwhile goal without short-cuts or instant gratification, attain more happiness and success in the long term. If my generation could just stick at a good but imperfect thing for a little while, without letting Instagram convince them that the grass is greener elsewhere, I think they could go really far and be really happy. But as I suggested earlier, social media has made perfect look so normal that 'good' feels disposable.

Most things of consequence in life are not simple or easy, they require work. Creating a career that makes you feel wholly satisfied is no different. I found five crucial elements to a 'dream job', ingredients that have been widely psychologically proven to increase human satisfaction. Income is not one of them. Nor are they as simple as 'finding your passion'.

1. ENGAGING WORK

Firstly, what really matters is not your salary, your status or even the industry but what you do day by day, hour by hour, second by second.

Engaging work is work that pulls you in, holds you and enchants you. It's the reason that for most people, like me, an hour spent doing paperwork or spreadsheets can feel mind-numbing while an hour playing a video game feels like no time at all: computer games have engagement at the heart of their design.

YOU WOULDN'T PLANT A SEED AND THEN DIG IT UP EVERY FEW MINUTES TO SEE IF IT HAD GROWN.

SO WHY DO YOU KEEP QUESTIONING YOURSELF, YOUR HARD WORK AND YOUR DECISIONS?

HAVE PATIENCE, STOP OVERTHINKING AND KEEP WATERING YOUR SEEDS.

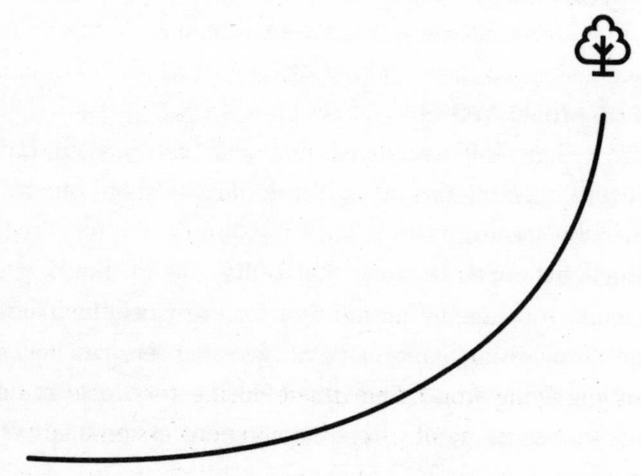

What makes the difference? Why are computer games absorbing while office admin is not? Researchers have identified four factors:

1. The freedom to decide how to perform your work
2. Clear tasks, with a clearly defined start and end
3. Variety in the types of task
4. Feedback – so you know how well you're doing

That said, playing computer games is not the key to a fulfilling life (and not just because you won't get paid). That's because you also need . . .

2. WORK THAT HELPS OTHERS

People, specifically younger people, seem mind bogglingly obsessed with 'changing the world'. They don't necessarily know how they want to change it, and upon questioning they don't always know which part they feel passionately enough about changing.

It appears that because people who change the world are globally admired (we erect statues that resemble them, movies are created about them and books are written and disseminated into classrooms detailing their life's work), as status-seeking beings, we think if we 'change the world' too, we'll receive the same level of admiration from the world and, more importantly, from ourselves to ourselves. That if we emulate those we admire, we'll admire ourselves.

Excuse my tangent, but this is another tormenting characteristic of living in such a connected, fake comparison-oriented and status-glorifying world. Our innate desire to achieve status has meant that so many of us conflate our professional admiration for someone else with our personal aspirations for ourselves.

Trying to imitate someone that you follow and admire, is a sure-fire way of never becoming someone that is followed and admired.

Our generation has confused their admirations with their aspirations.

Your idols did it their own way. If you want to achieve what they did, you'll have to too.

I so sincerely believe that we'll never find ourselves or our own happiness until we accept that we can't have anyone else's life but our own . . . and if we realise this, and focus on ourselves, then our lives will feel like more than enough.

Søren Kierkegaard, a Danish philosopher, wrote in his 1849 book *The Sickness unto Death* that a lot of misery in our lives stems not from depression, but rather from our alienation from our true self. He suggested that our growing self-awareness (that a connected world is forced to have), coupled with a profound dislike of who we are (the type of self-loathing that seemingly flawless influencers might force upon your lazy CEO mind), means we risk trying to escape who we actually are.

He illustrated in a simple flow chart that any attempt to abandon ourselves, successful or unsuccessful, would result in despair.

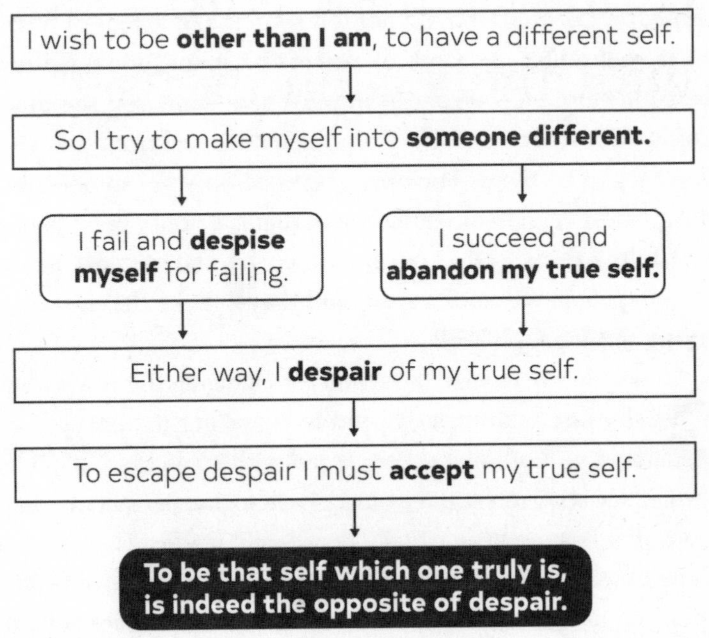

This is, of course, 19th-century philosophy, but it seems to hold an essential truth about the psychological risk of trying to be someone you're not. Maybe this is in part why the oppression of certain societal groups and minorities has caused so much misery and suicide.

Trying to become your idols isn't the answer either. They didn't follow in the footsteps of their heroes. There was no Bill Gates for Bill Gates to emulate; he had to carve his own individual path to find his own 'greatness'. Each of your idols' power is their uniqueness. They had the conviction to disagree with or look beyond the way the world was, the confidence to persevere and the strength to go against the status quo.

We celebrate their individuality, not their conformity, and the audacity of their beliefs – that black was equal to white, or their vision of pocket computers and connected worlds, or driverless cars and personal spaceships. These ideas could only come from people who did not follow in the footsteps of others. So if you're just in search of success or status, don't aspire to be your hero; stop trying to impersonate what you see others doing on Instagram. Learn from them and steal from them, but don't try to be them. The only great person you can become is the greatest version of yourself, and that is a pretty great person. The funny thing is that once you become the greatest version of you, people will look at you and they'll make the mistake of trying to be you as well.

So wanting to change the world for changing the world's sake is usually just bullshit social virtue signalling driven by social media and groupthink and rewarded with some kind of philanthropic social currency. But from a psychological perspective doing work that helps others actually does really matter. There's something called a 'helper's high' which describes the positive feelings someone has when they do something to help another person.

The more you aspire to be like an original thinker, creator or artist, the less chance you have of ever becoming an original thinker, creator or artist. Originality is not something you can replicate. It begins where replication ends.

The psychological theory is that giving and acts of kindness produce a natural mild version of a morphine high in the brain. Studies have consistently supported this theory. People who volunteer are less depressed and healthier than non-volunteers, and performing a random act of kindness makes the giver happier. A global survey found that those who help others the most are as satisfied with their lives as those who earn twice as much.

Helping others is by no means the only route to a meaningful career, but it's widely accepted by researchers that it's one of the most important. This doesn't mean you have to solely pursue charitable work or aim to 'change the world'; it can simply mean helping your colleagues or adding social responsibilities to your existing job or organisation.

Jobs that involve helping others score well in job-satisfaction rankings, as found in the General Social Surveys conducted from 1972 to 2006 (with 50,313 respondents):

Top occupations in job satisfaction

Rank	Occupation	Mean Score	% Very Satisfied
1	Clergy	3.79	87.2
2	Physical Therapist	3.72	78.1
3	Firefighter	3.67	80.1
4	Education Administrator	3.62	68.4
5	Painter, Sculptor-related	3.62	67.3
6	Teacher	3.61	69.2
7	Author	3.61	74.2
8	Psychologist	3.59	66.9
9	Special Education Teacher	3.59	70.1
10	Operating Engineer	3.56	64.1

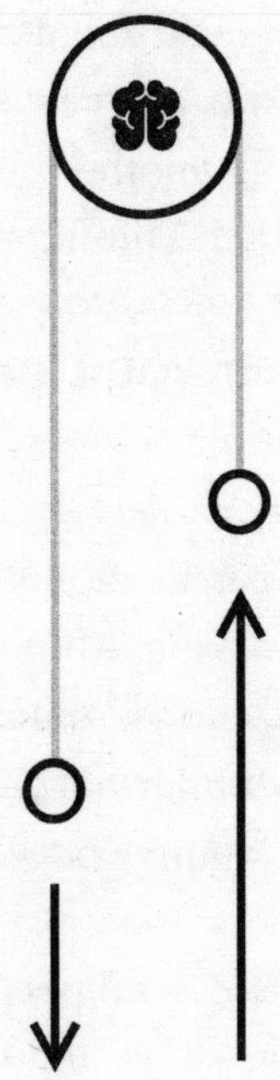

THERE IS NO EXERCISE BETTER FOR THE MIND THAN REACHING DOWN AND LIFTING ANOTHER PERSON UP.

Helping others is an innate feature of being human – if we didn't have that desire to help, and if it wasn't reinforced by endorphins in our brains, it seems unlikely that we would have been able to build supportive tribes and raise children – or ultimately to survive as a species.

As one of my most valued mentors said to me before they passed away: 'There is no exercise better for the mind than reaching down and lifting another person up'. It would appear that the more we lift others, the more we lift ourselves.

3. DON'T JUST DO WHAT YOU LOVE, DO WHAT YOU'RE GOOD AT

There's this thing called 'career capital' that people don't talk about enough. In short, career capital is anything that puts you in a better position to make a difference in your future career – such as skills, connections, qualifications and resources. Gaining career capital is important throughout your career, but especially when you're young, have a lot to learn and little reputation to rely on.

If you look at many successful people, say Oprah, Elon Musk or even Bono, they all started out in life by mastering one single industry and in doing so building a tremendous amount of career capital and reputation for themselves. They then leveraged this career capital to take on philanthropic, humanitarian and business interests.

The earlier you are in your career, and the less certain you are about what to do in the medium-term, the more you should focus on gaining career capital that's transferable to other sectors. I often refer to this as 'filling your buckets' when my more purpose-driven employees ask me what their purpose is.

At this stage in my own life, I'm pouring as much value as

I can into five key buckets that I will be able to leverage for life:

1. What I know (knowledge)
2. Who I know (network)
3. What I'm able to do (my skills)
4. What others think of me (reputation)
5. What I have (my resources)

Reputation matters more than we realise. My friend Brian in San Francisco told me of the day that he saw someone he loosely knew out on a morning jog. The man stopped to say hello to my friend and began zealously talking about launching rockets into space and landing on Mars. That man on that jog was Elon Musk. If I walked up to people on the street and enthusiastically told them I was going to Mars on a rocket that I was building, I would probably be sectioned. When Elon Musk said that, NASA gave him millions of pounds to do it.

That's career capital in practice, and that's usually achieved by doing something you're remarkably good at, not something you're merely passionate about doing.

Being good at your work does give you a sense of achievement, and achievement is a central ingredient to life satisfaction that has been repeatedly revealed by positive psychology. Ultimately, in the capitalistic and competency-driven world we live in, skill trumps interest. Even if I love painting, if I'm innately crap at it (and I am) but I pursued it as a career, I would likely end up not meeting other foundational needs like being able to feed myself. That's not to say you should only do work you're already good at. However, you should aim to pursue work you have the potential to get good at.

4. DON'T WORK WITH ARSEHOLES

Arseholes have the extraordinary ability to ruin almost anything – comedy shows, your commute in the morning, a movie at the cinema, your mental health and even a meaningful job.

You don't need to love everyone you work with but, according to numerous studies, perhaps the most important factor in job satisfaction is whether your boss and colleagues are supportive.

This doesn't mean you should only work with friends or those who will kiss your arse. People who are disagreeable are incredibly important in our work – they often give us the most valuable feedback provided they care about our interests (and we're willing to listen).

A bad boss, selfish colleagues or a toxic culture can ruin a 'dream' role, whereas agreeable workmates can make even mundane work enjoyable. When selecting a job, two of the most important questions you should consider is whether you think you will be able to make friends with these people, and if the culture of the organisation seems supportive.

'Don't work with arseholes'; and, if you need telling, don't be one either.

5. WORK–LIFE HARMONY

Society and social media loves to tell you how much work is too little work, and also how much work is too much work. It simultaneously peddles the 'you're not working hard enough' narrative alongside the 'you're working too hard you're going to burn out' narrative. Ignore both. Despite how much society, many educational institutions and some parents peddle the narrative that work is everything, this isn't true in any fathomable or scientifically justifiable way, and it's a notion we must resist. It's an idea created with someone else's agenda at heart – often in order to sell you something or to make you follow and admire some hustle-pornstar.

Conversely anyone that tells you that work doesn't matter or that working long hours is dangerous is being equally narrow-minded. Work matters but so does the rest of life. Creating meaning and fulfilment is an individual, fluid and multidimensional endeavour that we must all approach differently. I still work harder than anyone else I know, and I'm happy. I've got friends that don't 'work' at all and they're happy.

For me the most important thing has been finding my 'work-life harmony of needs;' finding harmony between my chosen responsibilities (personal ambitions), the things that cater to my basic needs (food, water and a place to live), my psychological-esteem needs (achievement, confidence and a feeling of progress) and my need for love, connection and belonging (family, romantic relationships and friendships).

Creating this harmony of needs is the thing that we should be promoting, aiming for and holding on to if we're fortunate enough to attain it. There is no perfect amount of hours to invest in each need, but there is a need for all of your needs to be met.

Society loves to tell you how much work is too little work, and how much work is too much work.

It simultaneously peddles the 'you're not working hard enough' narrative alongside the 'you're working too hard you're going to burn out' narrative.

Ignore both.

Chapter Ten

THE JOURNEY BACK TO HUMAN

AS I WRITE this chapter, I'm sat in an Indonesian jungle by a gloriously glistening river with the unobstructed glare of the sun overhead beating down on me. There's a perfect light breeze stroking my warm skin and the earthy, floral smell of the jungle's surrounding trees occupies my sinuses. I came here to live in a hut in the jungle in order to find the clarity of mind necessary to write this book, in order to reach my 'flow state', and as a necessary escape from the cold grey industrial backdrop of my home in the heart of New York.

As I sit here – and you may have experienced this if you've ever spent time in nature – I feel at peace. As the Stoics may have described it, I feel tranquil. It's hard to explain this in any other way than to say that I feel this is where I innately belong; my primitive survival-oriented senses that often use prehistoric devices like pain and discomfort as a useful way to guide me away from danger and towards safety seem to be telling me that this is where I 'should' be – the absence of discomfort is telling me that this might just be 'home'.

Inevitably, I'm going to have to return to the chaos of the

city where I live alone in a concrete box and where I, like many of my peers, spend up to 11 hours a day tapping away on a handheld illuminated piece of glass in order to communicate with the outside world – sometimes to instruct humans to bring me food, sometimes in an attempt to swipe my way to love, and often with no discernible aim at all.

Conveniently, I can use that illuminated piece of glass to call someone who will carry me in a large metal vessel (in total silence) from the lonely concrete box I live in to the high-intensity concrete box I work in, which means I can theoretically get through a whole day with virtually no movement.

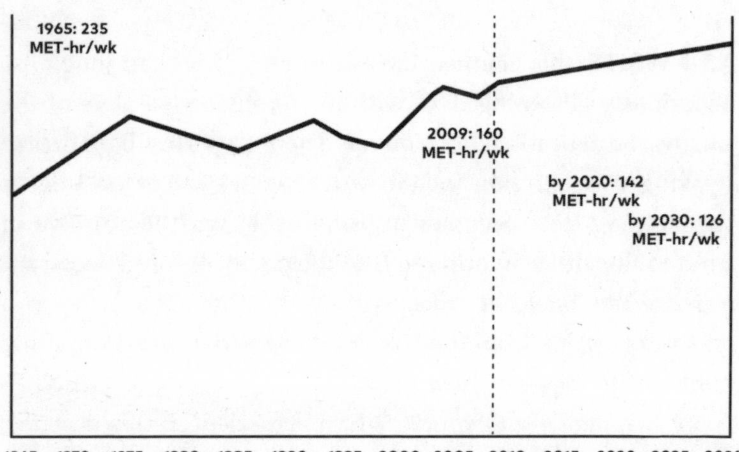

About 12,000 years ago we hunted in tribes to feed our communities on the grasslands of Africa. Now, I often sit alone in my boxers ordering tacos from the Mexican place one block away, filling the wait-time with as many swipes on Tinder as a trained thumb can perform. How the fuck is this a human way to live? Why are we doing this? Why have we so blindly accepted how Silicon Valley has 'optimised' the life out of our lives?

We're horrifically lonelier than ever before. We spend less time in nature than all previous generations, and we're more inactive now than at any time in human history. We're all patently aware and focused on catering to our physical needs (food, water, air) because if they go unmet, our bodies send us clear physical signals (hunger pains, thirst and other forms of discomfort) and then, if they continue to go unmet, we die.

But our psychological needs are invisible (community, human connection, free movement, meaning, nature), so we continue to employ technology to optimise against them in the name of convenience, saving time, our physical needs and becoming more 'successful'. Unsurprisingly, as is the consequence for unmet physical needs, our unmet psychological needs are sending us signals in an attempt to get us back to our tribes – feelings of loneliness, anxiety and depression – and we're ignoring them. We're telling people they're 'broken', they're crazy or, even worse, that everything is fine and just to get on with it.

Most of the 'new age' techniques that aim to improve your mental health are based on 'old age' principles of how life was 10,000 years ago.

We took a wrong turn and filled our lives with overstimulation, alcohol, caffeine, poor nutrition and loneliness.

It's time to turn back.

ALONE, UPSET AND DYING

This obsessive optimisation has made us the loneliest humans to ever live. Loneliness is currently at epidemic levels, further exacerbated by the COVID-19 pandemic and its global lockdowns. A recent study of 20,000 adults from Western countries found that nearly half of them feel like they are alone. Nearly half said they didn't have meaningful in-person social interactions on a daily basis, and half of them said they sometimes or always feel that their relationships aren't meaningful and that they're isolated from others.

Shockingly, one-fifth of those surveyed said they feel like they have absolutely no one to talk to. A large proportion of adults over the age of 45 suffer from chronic loneliness, while younger people (aged 18–37), ironically the most 'connected' generation ever, are the single loneliest generation in recorded history.

Clearly social networks aren't that social, and an internet connection doesn't guarantee human connection.

The loneliness epidemic is so bad that world leaders have been forced to intervene. In January 2018, British Prime Minister Theresa May appointed the world's first 'Minister for Loneliness', declaring that this was a decision taken to 'address the sad reality of modern life' and, in doing so, making the fight against isolation the official business of government. This news left me with a disturbing dystopian vision of the government screaming 'TALK TO EACH OTHER FOR FUCK'S SAKE' at us through public tannoys while we stand anxiously in lifts, underground trains and other public spaces.

I spend half my time in the US and half in the UK, and from my observations the British culture is by far the most introverted. In fact, our chronic social awkwardness and polite restraint feel like a defining characteristic of being British. From afar, one might conclude that we all hate each other, we're all socially inept or we suffer from a form of agoraphobia. Let me be clear, this is not the British people, it's the British culture. Send 10 British people to Southeast Asia with backpacks and they'll turn more strangers into friends in the first week than they will in a lifetime back home in London.

So what's the plan? How do we fix this? Well, The Minster for Loneliness produced an 84-page document called 'A Connected Society: A strategy for tackling loneliness'. And it proposes something called 'social prescribing' which would work like this: you visit your doctor with a physical complaint, but if feelings of isolation are suspected as an underlying cause of your symptoms, rather than just offer you medication they will instead refer you to a loneliness specialist whose job it is to 'work with people to produce a tailored plan to meet the person's well-being needs' and to help you 'overcome feelings of loneliness by connecting you to activities and support within their local area'.

This programme is designed to be a pressure valve for Britain's struggling National Health Service (NHS) after a plethora of global studies demonstrated that loneliness is linked to disease and early death and ranks as a causal factor alongside high blood pressure, obesity, alcoholism and smoking 15 cigarettes or more a day.

Former Surgeon General Vivek Murthy worryingly said: 'during my years caring for patients, the most common pathology I saw was not heart disease or diabetes; it was loneliness'.

I can't help but think that a loneliness specialist giving someone a plan and some activities to do is just papering over cracks, addressing the effect not the cause, and treating the problem but not the intrinsic design of society which is causing it. The truth is that if governments were to address the problem, it would likely require a complete overhaul of our current way of life, and god forbid it may happen at the expense of economic growth!

In a few weeks' time, when I reluctantly exchange this leafy jungle for the concrete jungle I call home, I'll once again become 21 per cent more likely to have an anxiety disorder and 39 per cent more likely to have a mood disorder – just by being in that lonely urban environment. Isn't that nuts? (No pun intended.)

In preparation for this book I travelled to meet Johann Hari, the renowned social analyst and distinguished author of *Lost Connections: Uncovering the Real Causes of Depression – and the Unexpected Solutions.* Drawing from more than a decade of research on the topic, he told me that one key reason for our need to be together in nature is our evolutionary past:

> "Our ancestors on the savannas of Africa were really good at one thing. They weren't bigger than the animals they took down a lot of the time, they weren't faster than the animals they took down a lot of the time, but they were much better at banding together into groups and cooperating. This was our superpower as a species – we band together; just like bees evolved to live in a hive, humans evolved to live in a tribe."

We're the first humans to disband our tribes and it is making us ill.

If I told you my mate Negra had a hunched posture, was expressionless and socially withdrawn, slept excessively during the daytime, lacked interest in fun, food, grooming and other individuals, while exhibiting poor attention to tasks, slow and sluggish behaviour and, at times, appeared to be anxious, without need of a university degree on the matter, you would unquestionably tell me that she was depressed. Everything I described was written into an extensive research piece produced by Dr Hope Ferdowsian, when she described the behaviour of Negra, a 36-year-old female chimpanzee who had been held alone in captivity for many years. But Negra isn't an exception. In one notorious study from the 1950s, University of Wisconsin psychologist Harry Harlow placed rhesus monkeys inside a custom-designed solitary chamber shaped like an inverted pyramid nicknamed 'the pit of despair'. Harlow wrote that the monkeys kept in isolation wound up 'profoundly disturbed, became emotionless – staring blankly into the distance, rocked in place for long periods, circled their cages repetitively and self-harmed frequently'. Those who had been in isolation the longest were the most irreversibly harmed. 'Twelve months of isolation almost obliterated the animals socially,' Harlow explained. These findings are particularly concerning as much of the Western world is currently living in isolation due to the COVID-19 pandemic. It makes you wonder how we will emerge from this period, what invisible harm has been caused and how it'll contribute to the loneliness epidemic.

This is a pattern observed across the animal kingdom, including in humans. In 1951, researchers at McGill University paid a group of graduate students to stay in small chambers equipped with only a bed and little sensory stimulation (for ethical and legal reasons we don't do studies like this these days). They could leave to use the bathroom, but that was all. The plan was to observe the students for six weeks, but the experiment ground to a halt after just seven days when the participants started losing their minds and every single participant dropped out. Nearly every student lost the ability 'to think clearly' while several others began to suffer bizarre hallucinations.

Our tribal ancestors
knew human connection,
simple living, exercise,
nature and water.

We know white walls,
busy cities, loneliness,
digital addiction,
insomnia, takeaway food
and fizzy drinks.

If you want to improve
your mental well-being, try
living a little more human.

Similarly, studies have found that roughly a third of solitary inmates in prison become 'actively psychotic and/or acutely suicidal'. Even small mammals like rats will lose their minds when they're held in captivity. A study by researcher Bruce K. Alexander observing the psychological impact of isolation and confinement offered rats a choice of heroin-infused water or normal water when they were held alone in small white cages. They found that those animals living in small white boxes would exhibit depressive behaviours, opting for the heroin water disproportionately more than those living in an open community (including the opposite sex), with exercise wheels, toys and other apparatus. The researchers named this manufactured rat paradise 'Rat Park'.

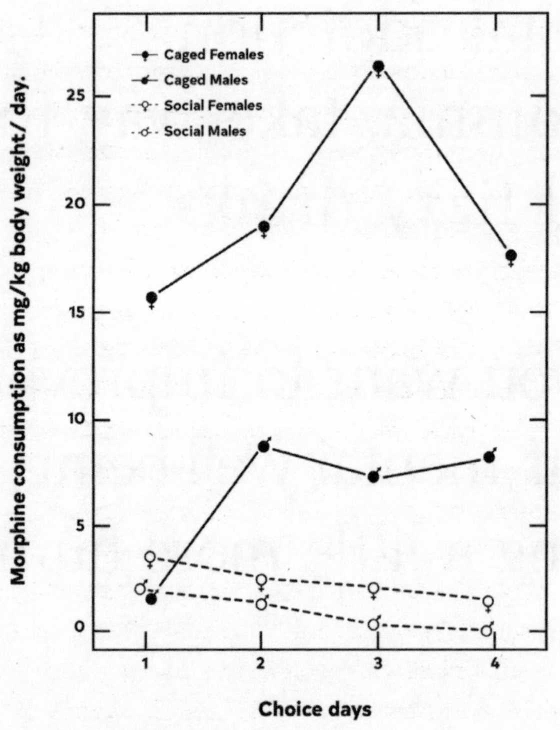

THREE BEST FRIENDS AND THEIR HUSTLE-PORN ADDICTION

I'm quite possibly the biggest culprit when it comes to self-isolation in the pursuit of success. At 18 years old I isolated myself for three years, completely snubbing anything that might resemble a healthy social life in order to build my first company (which failed miserably by the way). Over the next five years, as I built my next company, I'm sure I must have earned the world record for the most consecutive weekends alone in an office staring at a screen plus the record for the most nights spent sleeping in an office that you've just spent 16 hours working in. My unrelenting internal monologue was fuelled by the 'inspiration' of online hustle-pornstars and a toxic social media culture that glorifies anyone pretending to work really fucking hard or, conversely, anyone pretending to do the opposite. This reassured me that the harder I worked, the more stuff I would have, the richer I would become, the greater would be my status, the more women would like me and, therefore, the happier I would be. What an insecure, misguided man I was.

I looked down on those who weren't working themselves into the ground like me. Why were they spending time with friends and family when they could be making tons of money and 'climbing the ladder' like I was? Their balanced lifestyles made no sense to me – of course they didn't. When you stubbornly value career success above all else (like calling your mum, a meaningful relationship or your mental health) then 'all else' feels entirely pointless – like a permanent second priority. I was sure I was right and I was sure they were wrong.

Like Negra, the depressed chimpanzee, I was held captive by my own socially inspired miscalculation of my needs. I arrogantly and unknowingly rejected my psychological and emotional needs in the foolish pursuit of . . . social media needs,

I guess. And I was quick to encourage others to do the same. In fact, I think my success inspired all of my closest friends to do the same. It wasn't until two of my best friends and fellow hustlers started to break down in front of me that I asked myself some very important questions.

At 3am on a Tuesday morning in 2016 I was awoken by the unnerving sound of something smashing downstairs. At just 24 years old, my business partner, Dominic, and I were living in a six-bedroom countryside mansion behind a 12ft electric gate with a tennis court, cinema room, games room and much more – the stupid fucking decisions insecure men make to impress people! As I slowly proceeded down the stairs in my Calvin Kleins, ready for combat – but admittedly not dressed for it – I armed myself with a long wooden mop handle and prepared myself to joust (I guess) this daring intruder. I apprehensively flicked on the lights in the kitchen and, to my bewilderment, there was no burglar. Dominic was sat alone in the dark, drunk, at 3am on a Tuesday, with what appeared to be his second bottle of red wine. Without saying a word, I wrestled the bottle from his disobliging grip, poured the contents down the sink and dragged his limp body up to his bedroom on the third floor.

An hour later, after hearing another disconcerting sound, I ran upstairs to check on him and, to my horror, he was lying on his side covered in an unknown red liquid – his pillows, mattress and duvet dripping while he mumbled incoherently. I rushed across the room fearing the worst and flung his stained bedsheet off in one fell swoop . . .

'Oh, for fuck's sake, Dom!'

There he was. Naked. Smirking. And grasping a brand new half-spilled bottle of wine.

In the days that followed, the true nature of Dom's decaying mental health began to emerge. The isolation, lack of meaningful relationships and non-stop work at the expense of all else had caught up with him. He had unknowingly been a functioning alcoholic for some time. He was overweight, crippled with anxiety and he later admitted to fantasising about 'jumping in front of a train'. Like those rats trapped in stress-inducing cages, Dom was using his addiction to self-medicate the pain caused by years of unmet psychological and emotional needs.

We were best friends. We'd dropped out of university together, lived together for the best part of a decade, run two businesses together, travelled to every corner of the world together. We knew each other better than we knew ourselves – at least that's what I thought. He never told me how he was feeling, and I blame myself for that. He was too scared to show weakness to a 'tough guy' like me, who appeared to be unshakably resilient and immune to vulnerability. So he suppressed his emotions and tried to act invincible, not knowing that deep down I was just acting too. We had an impassioned heart-to-heart the next morning, admitting to each other the things that we had been both too scared to confess and, after several weeks of therapy, Dom completely transformed his life. He ended up losing 50lb, turned to a diet of healthy food, ran more marathons than I can count and gave up alcohol for good.

It wasn't until I got to know sober Dom that I realised I never really knew him.

Shortly after this, my second closest friend Anthony, an equally devout 33-year-old 'invincible' guy who believed in the same work-over-everything ideology I was sworn to, and who had spent every waking hour over the last four years doing absolutely nothing but working on his business – no friends, no family, no serious relationships, no socialising – called me out of the blue to tell me that he was suffering with severe anxiety, panic attacks and depression. He had been prescribed anti-anxiety medication and he was starting therapy that week.

For a second, think of your 'toughest' friend – the friend that might scoff at the idea of mental health like it's a pathetic myth and view anyone suffering with it as someone who simply needs to 'man up'. That was my friend Anthony.

Following these episodes, I took a long, hard look at myself – a long, hard look at the person hiding behind the manufactured public image I was broadcasting – and I asked myself how I was truly feeling? Not how the world thought I should feel based on my success. And I asked how I would feel in the future if this were to continue? It was clear something was missing and things had to change.

There's a fairly new social narrative emerging that hard work is inherently toxic – and that if you promote hard work as a successful person, you're being dangerously irresponsible. As tempting as it may be to conform with that narrative, I simply can't. I am not against hard work; there's little doubt in my mind that I will always work hard. I get tremendous fulfilment, stimulation and joy from the work I do and the sense of accomplishment it brings me – that too is part of being human. I also have to admit that I don't believe I would have achieved the level of success I have had I not worked excessively hard over the past years.

The issue isn't the hard work itself, it's what you work hard at the expense of. Dom, Anthony and I were unknowingly working hard at the expense of our psychological needs – at the expense of meaningful relationships, real human connection, exercise, seeing our families, love and everything in between. Just as our unmet physical needs will make us sick, our unmet psychological needs were making us sick too. We were living an unsustainably foolish and toxic naive fantasy.

We were winning at everything that didn't matter and losing at everything that did. We were wrong. They were right.

Over the past few years, all three of us have continued to bring balance to our lives and all three of us are unrecognisably happier. We jokingly describe this phase of our lives as the 'Journey Back to Human'. We prioritise socialising despite how pressing business may seem. We talk openly about our emotions to each other despite how vulnerable it makes us feel. We exercise religiously despite how tiring work can be. We spend time in nature despite how grim the weather gets. We call our mothers despite the lectures we get. And we've all fallen in love despite the odds.

Chapter Eleven

I JUST QUIT MY JOB

WHEN I STARTED writing this book, I was the 27-year-old CEO and founder of one of the world's largest and most illustrious publicly listed social media companies called Social Chain. Social Chain is my baby. I started the company at 20 years old, in the university I had dropped out of, at a desk that I had to pretend to be a student to use. I grew the company from a small idea to a business that has more than 700 team members around the world, generating $200 million in annual revenue and record profits. All the metrics that typically measure the success of a company were wildly outperforming our expectations – everything was apparently going great.

'So why the fuck did you quit, Steve?'

If that is what you're asking, you're not the only one.

Upon publicly announcing my resignation, I received thousands of messages, emails and comments telling me that I had made the wrong decision, that I was crazy and, in a few cases, urging me to reconsider. At first, the mass bewilderment, interrogation and speculation completely puzzled me, but of course they would, because I knew the reason for my decision, and to me it wasn't a tough one. When you understand the mental framework I've subconsciously used to make all of my major quitting decisions, you'll realise that I really had no decision.

I quit going to school at 16 (and was ultimately expelled), I quit university at 18, I quit every dead-end job I ever had within a few months. I then quit my first start-up aged 20 suddenly, and now I've quit Social Chain seemingly out of the blue. I'm perplexed when people refer to these decisions as 'brave' or 'risky' – to me, it would have been riskier not to quit, and because I have faith in my own rationale, none of these pivotal decisions were hard or felt brave. I was totally at peace on every occasion.

A FRAMEWORK FOR QUITTING

Much is written about the courage it takes to start – to start a new job, a new relationship, a new business or a new passion. Not enough is written about the equally important, equally courageous, equally confounding thing you usually have to do before you start something new – quitting the last thing.

Those horseshit, yet popular, clichés that tell you 'quitting is for losers' or that you must 'never give up' don't help anyone. They trap you in the toxic narrative that quitting is a weakness, an easy way out or, worse yet, that quitting is failure.

I assure you – quitting is for winners and quitting is a *skill*.

Knowing when to quit, change direction, leave a toxic situation, demand more from life or give up on something that you know in your heart isn't right and move on is a life-defining skill that people who find fulfilment, love and success – people who *win* at life – have intuitively mastered.

But it isn't easy. The greatest force stopping all of us going in search of the right thing is usually the gravitational pull from the wrong thing. The last thing. The safe thing.

Here is my Quitting Framework below. It's simplistic, lacking in nuance and deliberately general, but it's the fundamental framework that has subconsciously guided me through the pivotal moments in my life in an anxiety-free, decisive way. This is the first time I've written down or shared this framework, but I assure you this is the mental flow chart my mind has followed whenever I'm faced with a quitting decision.

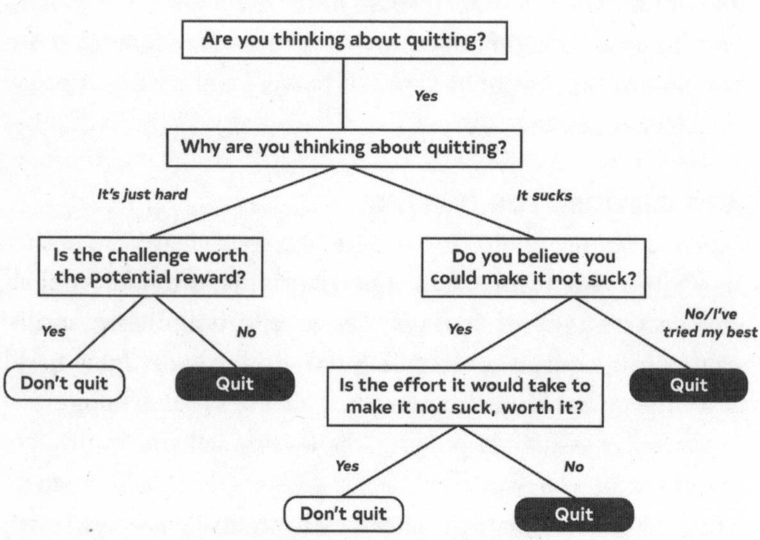

Every time I've quit, people have called me crazy. On one occasion my mother disowned me. Another time I was branded a failure in the national press. But every time, without fail, it's led me to more fulfilment, better love and higher success. Every single time. I have never regretted a major quitting decision. I seem to have always nailed both the decision and the timing of the decision.

Quitting even the most seemingly amazing thing, the greatest opportunity or the most comfortable situation and voluntarily throwing my life into uncertainty has always come easily to me. I credit this mental framework and the fact that when I reach the end of a pathway in the framework, I'm at peace with whatever the conclusion says must follow. I don't try to keep going. I don't talk myself out of it. I don't try to go back up the pathway in search of the answer I was 'hoping' for or the answer that will make my life easier today. I have faith in my logic, I have faith in myself and I find peace in the fact that this framework has never let me down.

I don't quit because things are just hard. In fact, the difficulty of a challenge often correlates to the reward it bears. Difficulty is a sign that I should keep going – that I'm actively choosing 'don't quit' in a 'growth moment' and so I search for increasingly harder challenges. My professional mission is to fill my life with difficult but worthwhile challenges. I tend to believe that if you do hard things now, you'll have an easy life later; and if you do easy things now, you'll have a hard life later. Going back to the point I made in Chapter Six about chaos being happiness and stability being chaos, this is my way of guaranteeing the chaos I need to be happy.

I do quit, though, because things suck, and I lose faith that I can stop them sucking and/or because the effort it would take to stop it sucking is no longer worth the reward on offer.

When I announced I was quitting my company, 60 per cent of the responses contained the question 'what's the plan?' or words to that effect, and to me this illuminated another important factor that prevents people quitting the wrong thing at the right time – the comfort-seeking need to have their next step perfectly figured out before they do so.

I had no plan. I just had a lot of faith in myself and a lot of faith in the rationale underpinning my decision.

CONTRARY TO POPULAR OPINION, QUITTING IS FOR WINNERS.

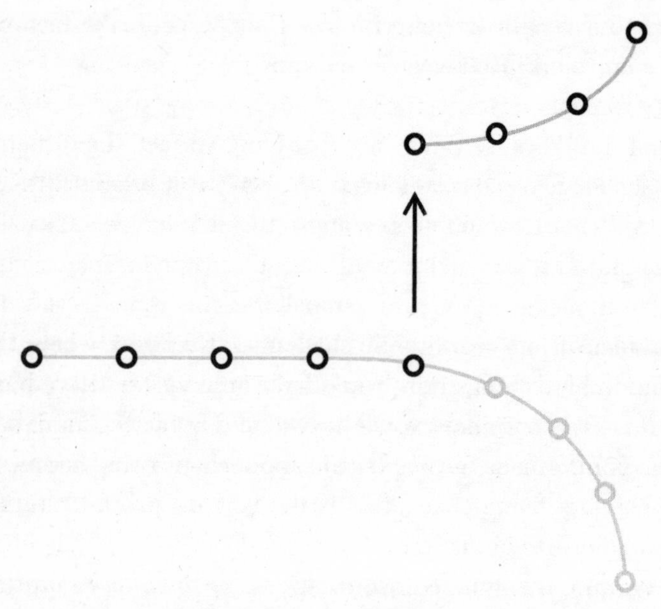

KNOWING WHEN TO QUIT, CHANGE DIRECTION, LEAVE A TOXIC SITUATION, DEMAND MORE FROM LIFE, GIVE UP ON SOMETHING THAT WASN'T WORKING AND MOVE ON, IS A VERY IMPORTANT SKILL THAT PEOPLE WHO WIN AT LIFE ALL SEEM TO HAVE.

Some people just can't seem to deal with any uncertainty in their lives, and time and time again they find themselves imprisoned in situations that kill their happiness, push them towards despair and gradually disintegrate their self-esteem. They don't realise that in their attempt to avoid uncertainty and the short-term discomfort it might bring, they're actually inadvertently opting for long-term misery. I believe that the happiness you'll find across all areas of your life – your work, your relationships and everything in between – will positively correlate to your ability to deal with uncertainty.

THOSE SPIDER MONKEYS AND A LESSON IN UNCERTAINTY

The first chapters of this book I wrote in a jungle in Bali in Indonesia. I'm now writing in a jungle in Costa Rica on the other side of the world. I'm serenely perched above the rainforest canopy in a beautiful plush wooden treehouse where I've been alone for the last few weeks. My only visitors have been the Costa Rican spider monkeys who swing by once a day to check in on me, steal my food and poop on my suitcases. A few days ago a monkey grabbed one of my Apple AirPods, presumably mistaking it for some kind of nut, and made his getaway. As I scampered towards him, he fearlessly leapt 10 metres off the treehouse down into the jungle and I watched helplessly as he swung from one tree to the next, grabbing one branch, swinging himself forward, letting go and optimistically flying through the air before grasping the next.

Despite their criminal behaviour, these monkeys can teach us all a lesson about the importance of embracing uncertainty. After all, if they don't take the leap, if they don't let go of the last branch and propel themselves into that brief moment of uncertainty before grasping the next, they would not move forward at the speed they need to in order to survive.

IF YOU CAN'T HANDLE UNCERTAINTY,

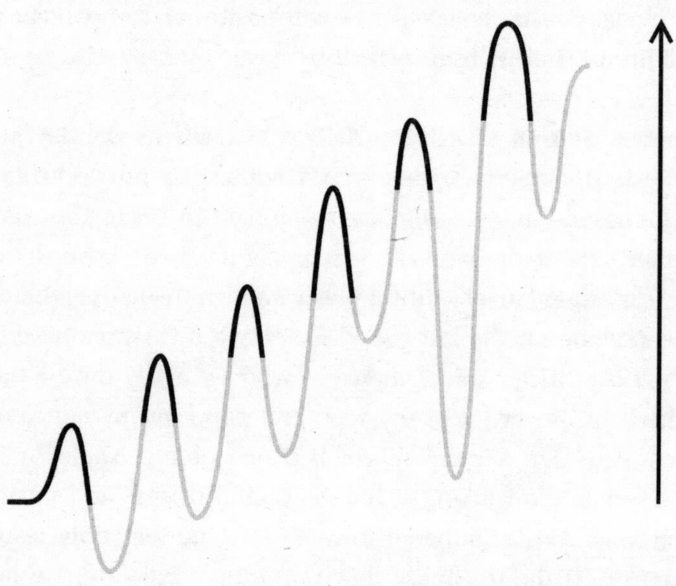

YOU CAN'T HANDLE GROWTH.

Similarly, the human experience is not linear. It is a series of unexpected chapters, hurdles and pivots – it's an assault course that guarantees even the most competent contender occasional bad news, bad decisions and bad fortune. You are guaranteed to make bad choices until the day that you die, and that's fine because that's life. For those who have the courage to choose uncertainty over the certain misery of a current situation, bad choices in your past become nothing more than a 'mistake' that served to help you make good decisions in the future. They become valuable, advantageous and regret-free lessons in your rear-view mirror, as you spider monkey yourself away from them and on to a better, stronger branch.

For those who unavoidably make bad decisions but struggle to find the courage to spider monkey their way out because they can't deal with uncertainty, or 'it might hurt someone's feelings'

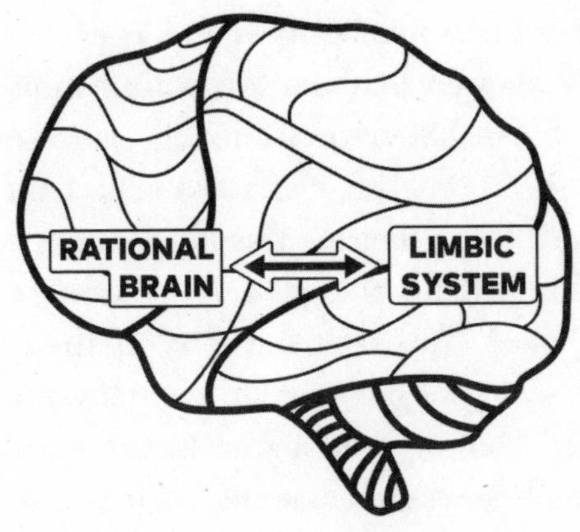

or because they 'don't have a perfect plan', one unrectified mistake piles on top of the last and after a decade of indecision they find themselves living a life they loathe in a place that makes them unhappy, in a loveless relationship and working a depressing 9–5 job with colleagues who make them miserable.

Uncertainty is the gap between your current miserable situation and an unknown happier position. It's a place you have to travel through time and time again, in all areas of your life, if you want more fulfilment, more love and more success than you're currently getting. It's the most vulnerable place on earth – the lights are off, there's no sat nav and the destination is unknown. However, when you work through my Quitting Framework and it becomes clear that your current situation sucks and is leading you towards inevitable unhappiness, you must embrace the fact that the certain misery of your current situation will never be a better option than the uncertainty you'll encounter as you search for more, better, happier.

Our brains are hardwired to react to moments of uncertainty with fear. In one brain study, a Caltech neuroscientist scanned people's brains as they were forced to make increasingly uncertain choices – the same kind of choices we're forced to make on a regular basis in life, business and love.

The study showed that the less information the subjects had before making their decisions, the more irrational and erratic their decisions became. You'd expect the opposite to be true – you'd think that the less information available then the more calm, careful and rational we would be before we make our choices. This isn't the case. As the uncertainty of the different scenarios increased in the study, the participants' brains shifted control over to the limbic part of the brain which is the place where emotions, such as anxiety and fear, are generated. (see the illustration on the previous page.)

This neurological wiring, which has remained the same for thousands of years, was handy when we were cavemen and women straying into an unfamiliar area at night.

UNCERTAINTY IS THE GAP BETWEEN YOUR CURRENT MISERABLE SITUATION AND AN UNKNOWN HAPPIER POSITION.

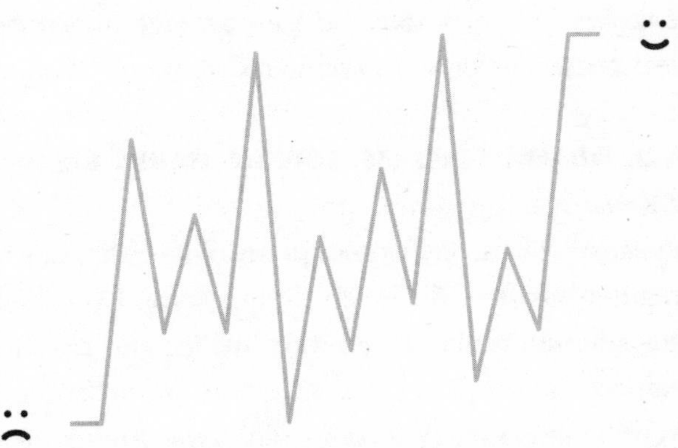

IT'S A PLACE YOU HAVE TO TRAVEL THROUGH TIME AND TIME AGAIN, IN ALL AREAS OF YOUR LIFE, IF YOU WANT MORE FULFILMENT, MORE LOVE AND MORE SUCCESS THAN YOU'RE CURRENTLY GETTING.

Back then, being fearful in uncertain situations ensured our survival but, today, these mechanisms aren't helpful in the context of the world we live in and the daily decisions we have to make.

It has been clinically proven that successful people are able to override this innate mechanism and shift their thinking to a more rational place. This requires a significant amount of emotional intelligence (EQ), and so it's no wonder that among the more than 1 million people who have been tested by TalentSmart, a world-leading EQ assessment company, 90 per cent of the top performers have high EQs, they undoubtedly live happier lives and they earn an average of $28,000 more per year than their low-EQ counterparts do.

BARACK OBAMA TOLD ME HOW HE MAKES BIG DECISIONS

At 14 years old, I sat on the floor of my oldest brother's bedroom with tears of joy and disbelief in my eyes as I watched Barack Obama win the 2008 US election to become the first black president.

Twelve years later, at 26 years old, I was invited to speak at a 15,000-capacity venue in São Paulo, Brazil, alongside the man himself – an 'is this even real?' moment.

Fanboying aside, even as the CEO of a multinational organisation, the decisions I've faced pale in comparison to the decisions a world leader tasked with defending a nation of 350 million people, managing the world's greatest economy and directing the world's largest military must face, every single day.

In our daily lives, many people habitually obsess, agonise and procrastinate over comparatively inconsequential decisions like what outfit to wear or which person to date. There is clearly a huge disparity between the significance of your daily decisions and those of the President of the United States, but I've never believed this means the principles that guide those decisions have to be any different – in fact, the fundamental structure should, in theory, be transferable.

The choices we make and the timing with which we make them are everything. Our lives today are a consequence of decisions we made a year ago and our lives a year from now will be a consequence of the decisions we make today. So how did Obama make his decisions? How did he make the decision to launch a strike to take out the world's most abominable terrorist, Osama Bin Laden? In Brazil, I had the once-in-a-lifetime opportunity to find out and here's what he said: 'I only dealt with the hard stuff. If it was an easy problem to solve, or even a moderately difficult but solvable problem, it would not reach me because, by definition, somebody else would have solved it by then; but if it was a really difficult problem, or a seemingly lose–lose scenario, it landed on my desk.'

He went on to say: 'The first step to making those hard decisions is being comfortable with the fact that you're not going to make a perfect decision – not all the time, maybe never; and understanding that you're dealing with probabilities, so that you don't get paralysed trying to think that you're going to actually solve it perfectly.'

He continued, 'Once I have all the information, and I'm confident that I understand the challenge, if I could get to 51 per cent probability on a decision, having consumed all of the available information, then I would make that decision and be at peace with the fact that I had made the best decision I could with all the available information I had.'

There's a renowned psychologist called David Dunning who is known for studying stupidity, and his work illuminates how the smartest people think, predict and make decisions.

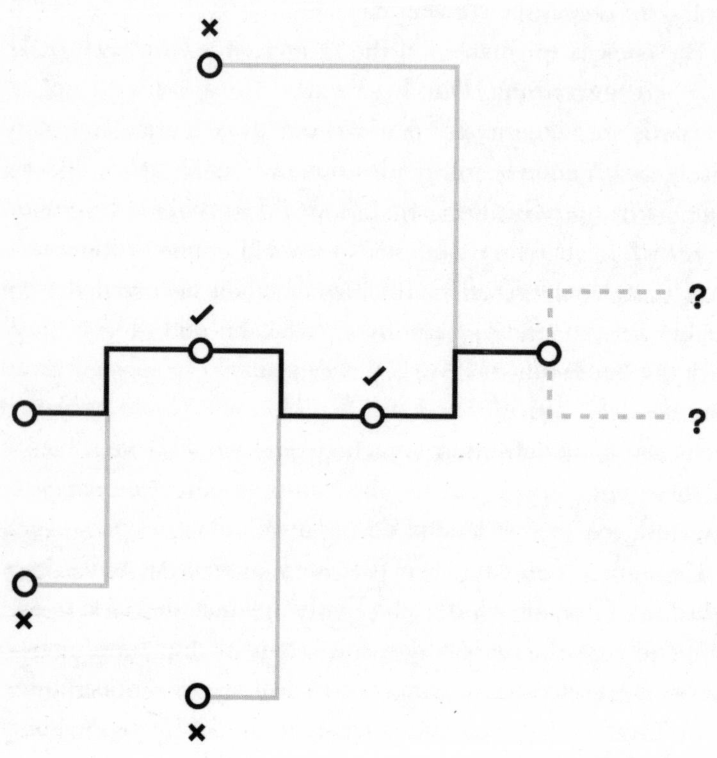

OVERTHINKING AND THE PROCRASTINATION IT CREATES STEMS FROM TRYING TO MAKE PERFECT DECISIONS IN A WORLD WHERE PERFECT DECISIONS ONLY EXIST IN HINDSIGHT.

Dumb people, he recently opined, see the world in black and white and make emotional decisions whereas smart people think in probabilities. Strong decision-makers ask: 'Not, "Will X or Y occur?" but, "What is the chance of X or Y occurring — 10, 50, 80 per cent?"'

Obama is evidently a smart decision-maker. He turns to reason, logic and probability in situations where others turn to emotion or 'gut instincts'. In fact, his predecessor President George W. Bush, who was famous for making one of the worst foreign-affairs decisions in US history when he invaded Iraq looking for chemical weapons (that were not there), once boasted, 'I'm not a textbook player. I'm a gut player.' That explains a lot.

Overthinking (and the procrastination it creates) stems from trying to make perfect decisions in a world where perfect decisions only exist in hindsight. A 51 per cent decision, is enough to be at peace. Know that 100 per cent doesn't exist. If you can make more decisions at 51 per cent you'll get feedback faster, learn faster and progress faster towards your desired outcome. If you continually endeavour to reach 90–100 per cent certainty on key decisions, not only will you be plagued by procrastination, apprehension and indecisiveness, but you'll lose time, the chance to learn and you'll miss important opportunities.

Chapter Twelve

KEEPING YOUR PLANE IN THE AIR

AS I LOOKED down at my phone, I felt an all-consuming vengeful wrath come over me. I had just received a message from an acquaintance telling me that the girl I had been casually dating for the previous six weeks, with whom I had ended things a few days earlier, had just, apparently, been with someone else. Instantaneously, and without consultation, my brain started thinking about all the ways I was going to confront her and reproach her.

I've spent my life in high-pressure business situations where bad news is both unpredictable and frequent. I've had adversaries in business who have tried to maliciously take down our company on many occasions and there have been days when the entire world and media have seemingly turned against me with false accusations and criticism.

If you run a well-known global organisation for seven years and you have a public profile, it's inevitable that unpredictable chaos, duplicity and bad news will become an unpleasant but recurring part of your life.

Because of this, I've been able to develop an unwavering and dependable sense of calm in the most ferocious moments of disruption so it's rare that anything moves me to the point that I can't control my thoughts, reactions and feelings. It's also dangerous. The damage you can do with the slip of a finger, an ill-considered tweet or a flippant reaction when you have millions of followers online, 700 employees and some of the world's biggest brands as your clients is quite terrifying. Composure really *really* matters.

But in that moment, as I stood in my kitchen staring down at the message on my phone, composure eluded me.

I tried to disregard the news. I couldn't. I tried listening to music to change my state of mind but it didn't work. I tried telling myself not to think about it . . . nice try. Hoping that this intense ball of energy inside me might dissipate with exercise, I got up, put on my sneakers and decided to go for a run. The run was only good at giving me more time and space to think, and during that thinking time my mind engaged in an aggressive wrestling match between two opposing trains of thought.

The first train of thought, which I'll call 'reason', said: 'Steve, you dumped this girl out of the blue; you hurt her, you knocked her self-esteem. The chances are, she went out and did this to try to restore the pride that your decisions took from her. She isn't in a relationship with you, she is within her rights to be with whoever she wants to. You cannot confront or antagonise her for this, let it go, move on.'

The second train of thought, which I'll call 'ego', said: '@%$#! ^*%$#! YOU NEED TO TELL HER RIGHT NOW THAT YOU KNOW AND THAT YOU THINK SHE'S A &%#! SHE THINKS YOU WILL NEVER FIND OUT BUT YOU CAUGHT HER, AND ONCE YOU'VE TOLD HER, TEXT ALL THE HOT WOMEN YOU KNOW, GET THEM TO COME OVER AND LET'S GIVE

HER A TASTE OF HER OWN MEDICINE. HOW DARE SHE? PLAN YOUR REVENGE IMMEDIATELY.'

Attached to the voice of my ego, there was another unspoken, insecure narrative that lingered somewhere in the shadows without conscious acknowledgement. That voice whispered, 'Maybe she didn't really like you? Maybe you're not enough? Prove to her, and yourself, that you are enough. Show her that it's her loss.'

As I ran through the streets of London, it became clear that the voice of my ego was winning the battle. I turned around and ran back to my house just 15 minutes after setting off. When I got back, I went upstairs, lay on my bed and started plotting how I would realise the egotistical justice I was seeking. I drafted a message to send to her – it was petty, immature and emotional. My ego approved. The damage it would do to her felt like it would somehow repair a wound somewhere inside me. Chaos, destruction and revenge were clearly the antidote and it felt like I was stood on the verge of a great victory.

And then the phone rang.

It was my best mate, Anthony, my ex-hustle-pornstar mate I mentioned earlier. Before he could tell me why he called, I blurted out 'Someone's just messaged me saying they've seen xxxx with someone,' and told him what had happened, how I was feeling, and I read to him the resentful message I was planning on sending her.

Anthony sighed, 'You're being an idiot, mate. Stop. You won't achieve anything by sending that message. She really liked you, she did. And you dumped her. It's probably just her misguided way of trying to move on from you. Remember, you didn't want her, you rejected her. She didn't reject you. She likes you.'

If you want to avoid making the same mistake twice, make more decisions based on your past memories and less decisions based on your current emotions.

—

Anthony's objective advice matched the voice of reason in my mind, but the voice of reason, however logical it had been, just couldn't seem to overpower my ego. Anthony's reminder – that she didn't do this because she didn't want me, but because I had ultimately rejected her – was, as embarrassing as it is to admit, the reason I decided to postpone my retaliation that night. Shortly after our phone call, I drifted off to sleep.

By the next morning, my ego had seemingly subsided, and the voice of reason was back in control. I no longer felt the need to retaliate; the inexorable feeling of animosity from the night before had dissipated. Although I still felt disappointed and a bit gutted, I understood the situation and that it would be wrong to criticise her considering the context. I decided no reaction or response were most certainly the best answer.

I've reflected deeply on why the words 'she really liked you' and 'you rejected her' mattered above all others, and I think I know why. When someone cheats on or dumps us, or when we feel rejected in any context, it isn't the action itself that harms us, it's the stories we then subconsciously tell ourselves about ourselves because of the rejection that ultimately do all the damage. A deliberate act of rejection is a brutal assault on our self-esteem and our sense of self-worth. It's as if someone else's actions have proved to us, with irrefutable certainty, what we always feared – that we are not enough. That we are not pretty enough, smart enough or worthy enough.

We all tend to think, and like to think, that we're stronger, more confident and more resilient than we actually are. Especially men, and especially me. I more than anyone have always thought I was somewhat emotionally vacant and psychologically robust. The truth is, our sense of self-worth can be such a sensitive thing, especially when we expose it to feedback and scrutiny in the context of an audition, job interview or public piece of work, and even more so when we expose it to the chance of bitter rejection in romantic relationships. Our work, our talents and our love are all crucial building blocks in the composition of our self-esteem.

If you have low self-esteem, even the slightest incidence of rejection can be completely devastating. From my observations, it appears that the time it takes someone to recover from a rejection directly correlates to both the magnitude of the rejection but also to how low their self-esteem was before the act of rejection. Sadly, those with low self-esteem go to great lengths to avoid the possibility of rejection. They habitually avoid promising opportunities, engage in self-disparaging behaviour and talk themselves out of the chance of romantic love.

I have a relatively high self-esteem – although clearly not impenetrable. My friend's words and some sleep helped to restore my self-esteem to a level sufficient for reason to regain control of my cognitive behaviour, to extinguish my ego and for me to let the situation go.

It's as if I was the pilot of a large commercial plane flying through the sky, and upon receiving the message that my former girlfriend had been with someone else, emotional terrorists had assaulted me, the very reasonable pilot, and forcefully hijacked the plane, locking me out of the cockpit. To these kamikaze terrorists, victory was crashing the plane, which evidently would have only harmed me and others. In situations like this – which we all encounter frequently in work, love and life – our central objective has to be to summon the self-awareness, perspective and rationality that we need in order to coerce these terrorists out of the cockpit and to regain control of the plane before we do something we'll regret.

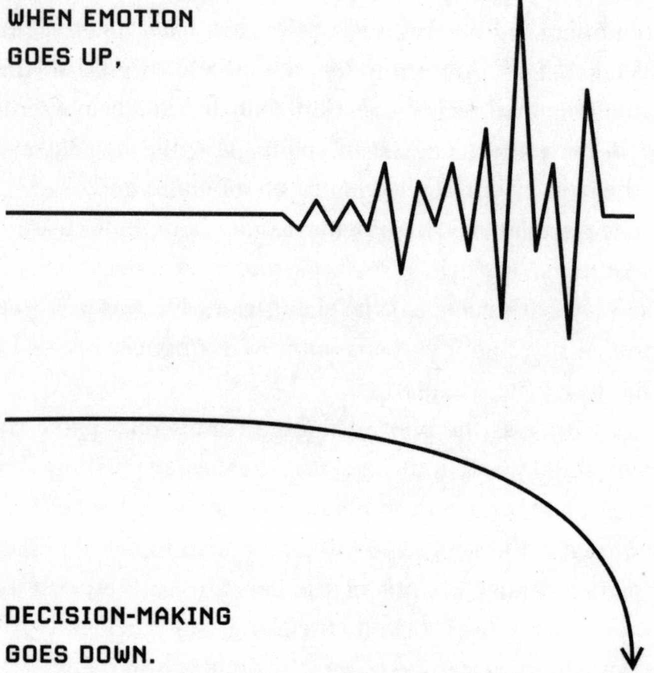
WHEN EMOTION
GOES UP,
DECISION-MAKING
GOES DOWN.

In moments like this, your brain will lie to you because a bruised ego will value short-term 'victory' over long-term outcomes. If you feel an urge to 'win', take revenge or protect your ego, then your rational mind is no longer in control. Do not listen.

The best reaction in high-emotion, ego-wounding situations is nearly always no reaction, but in the moment, that feels impossible. When emotion goes up, decision making goes down. So firstly you need to have the self-awareness to know that your emotions, ego or bruised self-esteem have taken control, and you must do everything in your power to prevent those forces making the decision on your behalf, in that moment.

If you can't seem to achieve that, like I couldn't, then consult a friend, pause, wait, sleep and tell yourself that you will address this in the morning. Do whatever you need to do to keep the plane in the air.

If the terrorists win, and the plane crashes, you will regret it.

Chapter Thirteen

FLYING YOUR PLANE THROUGH A TORNADO

IT WAS 8AM on 19 August 2015. I was in my car cruising down an empty motorway rapping along to Drake's brand new album 'If You're Reading This It's Too Late'. In my rear-view mirror, I could see my business partner, Dominic, in his car. I knew today was going to be a good day. After two years of hard work, sleepless nights in the office and nerve-racking uncertainty, our business was finally showing real signs of momentum. We'd just landed a series of global clients and recorded our best-ever commercial quarter to date and to celebrate, we'd organised a team building day with all 100+ team members from our Manchester office, which was to kick off with a game of paintball in the countryside.

As I pulled up at a set of traffic lights my music was interrupted momentarily by an incoming call. The caller ID read 'Dom', which was surprising because me and Dom almost never called each other – we always sent voice notes or text messages – plus he was just behind me and we were minutes from our destination so presumably whatever he had to say could wait. I inquisitively peered into my rear-view mirror to look for him and I caught a brief glimmer of his face. He looked like he had seen a ghost – he was staring into his phone, mouth wide open and frozen like an ice sculpture.

I accepted his call, 'What's up?' I opened.

'Check your email!' he interjected. I flicked over to the email app and saw an email from Sebastien Sobel. Sebastien had approached us a few months earlier about investing millions of pounds into our company. After a few trips to Milan, months of negotiations and weeks of strenuous due diligence, we were just days away from closing an investment deal that we knew would change everything for us.

Sebastien's email simply read: 'Assume this wasn't for me . . .!'

Re: Due Diligence Checklist
August 19, 2015 at 8:01 AM

Assume this wasn't for me...!

Perplexed and curious as I couldn't recall myself or Dom emailing him, I scrolled up to see what he was replying to. Here is what I saw:

> On 19 Aug 2015, at 07:53, Dominic
> <> wrote:
>
> Forwarded this messages to you Lisa. Can this guy not take a hint or what ? Just tell him Steve's busy on that day or that he's away on "business" we've got more important things to focus on

This was an email sent to Sebastien, about Sebastien, from Dom's email address that was supposedly meant to be sent to my then PA, Lisa. The email showed Dom telling Lisa that Sebastien needs to 'take a hint' (presumably implying that we didn't want to go ahead with the investment deal) and asking Lisa to lie to him about my whereabouts.

'For fuck's sake, why did you send that?' I barked through the car's speakerphone.

'I didn't . . . I promise I didn't. I didn't!' Dom zealously insisted.

Silence ensued. I know Dom. I've known him for seven years and lived with him for four years. He is the nicest, politest guy I know and he would never, ever, say something like that. And he doesn't lie to me. I didn't question his response for a millisecond. Nobody else had access to his emails. I could see that the email was sent at 7:53am – we woke up at 7am and left the house at 8am sharp. At 7:53am we were eating breakfast together and talking about the day ahead. There is no way this email was sent by him.

'Pull over and change your email password!' I ordered as I hung up the phone. Drake's 'If You're Reading This It's Too Late' resumed its passage through my speakers – it was only in hindsight that I noticed the irony of the album name.

But I could no longer hear the lyrics to the songs, my surroundings were a blur. My mind had zoned out and switched into some kind of autopilot mode. A sense of concentration and calm intensity fell over me as I began to compile the mental checklist of things that I knew I had to do next. Secure Dom's email address, confirm that all other email addresses on our server were secure, change all company passwords, triple-check we have two-factor authentication installed across our email server, speak to the host of our server to find out where this email came from, consult a cybersecurity firm on how we prevent this happening again, call Sebastien immediately to candidly explain the situation, call him again once I have the evidence from our server and call my lawyer to seek legal advice.

I figured I would pull up to paintball, adopt my frequently worn 'everything's okay' mask in front of what I knew would be an excited team, tell them to get started without me and then slip back to my car to begin the investigation and exoneration process.

As I raced towards the paintball centre, Drake's voice was abruptly silenced once again by a second incoming call from Dom. Before he could speak, I barked, 'I'm going to fix it.' An unexpected moment of silence fell as Dom timidly replied, 'There's more.'

I pulled up on the side of the road alongside a farm immediately. Glaring down into the email app on my phone I could see that our single largest client – one of the world's biggest movie studios that we had signed a potentially multi-million pound deal with just one month earlier – had emailed us with the following:

'Consider the campaign cancelled.'

Scrolling up I could see that they had received a disparaging email from Dom's email address at 6:32am.

Once again, this offensive email was apparently meant to be sent by Dom to Lisa, but he had seemingly accidentally copied in the client in question.

The potential magnitude of the situation began to dawn on me. It was 8am; most people weren't awake or on email yet. If we'd already had two replies like this, I feared how many others had received these precise and targeted malicious emails. The specific details included made it clear that the hacker had done their research – they had evidently read multiple conversations in Dom's inbox in order to produce an email that was personal, indefensible and destructive.

As I turned into the car park at the paintball centre, I was greeted by the sight of my joyful, energetic and smiling colleagues. The sense of excitement and eagerness for the day ahead was palpable. As I pulled into a spot as far from the crowd as I could be, Lisa looked over, waved cheerfully, and began striding towards me. I waved back disingenuously with my right hand, discreetly locking the doors with my left. As she got closer to the car I gestured to her that I just needed a minute of privacy and that I would be over in a second.

Grabbing my phone I refreshed my inbox. To my absolute horror, I had received two angry emails from two of our biggest clients. They had also received offensive personal emails from Dom's email address between 5:30 and 6:30am. These were consistent with the others, containing an unbelievably specific personal insult that was apparently meant to be sent to Lisa, but had accidentally copied them in. The theme of their responses was also consistent: they were offended and seeking to cancel our contract immediately.

I looked at the jubilant crowd of people in front of me and then back down to the chaos unfolding in my inbox. I knew what I had to do.

I stepped out of the car with a calm look on my face, walked over to the waiting crowd and gestured them to quiet down so that I could speak to them as a group.

'Hey everyone, we've had a little security incident with our email server, so unfortunately we're all going to have to head back to the office for a little while so that we can resolve it. If everyone could jump in a car and meet me back at the office that would be great.'

The lively car park fell into silence as people began to process my words. They stared at me, looked over at each other and then, after a few moments as comprehension of the enormity of the situation dawned, they began to scuttle quickly towards their cars. They didn't question me because they knew me – and they knew I wouldn't say something like this, on a day like this, lightly.

I arrived back to the office first and set up camp with Dom in a large glass meeting room in the middle of the office. We began to work through the checklist of immediate actions we knew we had to take in order to secure our servers and understand the scale of the attack. Once the team had returned to the office, I made a second announcement detailing what had happened, what we knew so far and what steps I was taking to rectify it.

As I've always said to Dom, when you're a leader and are delivering sensitive news to your team, it isn't just what you say that your team hear – it's how you say it. Fortunately, I've always been an expert at delivering difficult news in a way that makes the receiver feel like it isn't difficult news. I was calm, confident, unemotional and assertive. Years later, team members would tell me that they knew something was seriously wrong, but they didn't worry because of the tone of my announcement.

In the hours to come, we would receive over 20 furious, shocked and vengeful emails and phone calls from our major clients.

The detail given in the emails, referring to past and future campaigns, plus the personal insults used were extremely damaging. Most of our long-standing and valued clients just didn't believe that Dom had been hacked.

Large corporations, huge entertainment companies and major movie studios all cancelled the upcoming work we had agreed with them, and let me know that I was a 'coward' and a 'liar'.

You'll never prevent all chaos.

But you can learn to find your calm in any chaos.

I purposefully chose to station myself in the large panoramic glass boardroom that looked out on the office floor. People stood around their desks – still wearing their multi-layered paintball outfits – in anticipation of further instruction. I knew people would be speculating, whispering and concerned. I figured if they could see me and I was maintaining a calm demeanour, it would help to eliminate some of their potential anxiety. As the emails, calls and cancellations rolled in from our clients, and our hard-earned partnerships disintegrated one by one, the boardroom began to feel more and more like a bunker. I was just 22 years old and I was in the middle of a potentially fatal shitstorm, trying to navigate my way through one of those rare bouts of unexpected chaos that life just can't prepare you for.

I knew my team had just lost the majority of their clients, that our investor would potentially pull out, and that we weren't in a healthy enough financial position to survive this. I didn't even know if the attack had ended but whoever had done this to us would be ecstatic at the damage they had caused.

But honestly, I didn't feel sorry for myself; I wasn't angry and I wasn't worried. Unexpected chaos and bad news had been a recurring part of my life for many years – as the CEO of a rapidly growing company, that is quite frankly unavoidable. You can't stop them; you just have to develop mechanisms to deal with them. Admittedly, I hadn't experienced a day as turbulent as that day before. I couldn't 'prepare' for it, but through my combination of nature, nurture and experience, I naturally always turn to logic, reason and rational thinking in moments of chaos.

In these moments, there's something inside me that automatically becomes totally unemotional, incredibly focused and relentlessly fixated on solving the problem at hand. Nothing else matters, and I will not entertain anything other than rational solutions from rational people. Deep down, almost innately, I think I realise that anger, self-pity and other potent emotions are nothing more than a distraction from solving the problem. They are not my friends; they will interfere with my ability to think clearly and, in professional moments like these, I do not allow them access to the cockpit. In moments of chaos like this, when emotions go up, intelligence goes down. Evidently, I respond much more effectively when you attack my company than I do when a random message from a relative stranger reveals something about a girl I hardly knew that attacks my self-esteem and ego!

Realising that the harsh barrage of emails, calls and messages was not going to end any time soon and that I couldn't keep my team waiting much longer, I made another company-wide announcement in which I optimistically shared the progress we had made on the situation, what I was going to do next to appease our clients and secure our server, and I asked the team to take the day off and pick up their work from home. Privately, I informed the senior directors of the magnitude of the situation and instructed them both collectively and individually on what they could do to help me and to keep the team protected.

I sat in that bunker with Dom until the early hours of the morning. We had managed to collect evidence from our server that proved the emails were sent from an android phone in another city between the hours of 5am and 8am. In total 37 emails had been sent; the hacker had then tried to delete them from our server in an attempt to make it harder to resolve.

Respond, don't react.

I wrote a detailed statement outlining what we knew, the timeline of events and some of the key names that had been targeted. I shared it with all 37 contacts that had received one of these malicious emails and I apologised sincerely to everyone. Although it wasn't our fault, as CEO I still felt a great sense of responsibility. To me, what I had done mattered just as much as what I hadn't done to prevent it. I hadn't taken email security as seriously as I could have, I hadn't put systems in place to safeguard executive communication channels and I hadn't sought professional advice on wider data security issues.

We lost roughly 80 per cent of our clients that day. The 20 per cent that stayed with us were those who knew us personally, were familiar with our characters and who Dom really was. Some of the clients that cancelled their contracts with us did so not because they didn't believe us, but because their legal departments felt our security systems were too weak and that we posed the threat of a potential data breach in the future.

The days to come were deeply challenging for our team. I remember finding a young team member crying in the hallway because all of the clients she had fought so hard to win had cancelled their contracts, and one of them had sent her a flurry of passive-aggressive insults for good measure. It was as if that one day sent us straight back to the starting line. Our commercial momentum was gone, our team were understandably disheartened, and I knew that, as things stood, I would not be able to make payroll next month.

For some reason, I didn't ever acknowledge the pressure of the situation, I didn't show my emotions (not even to Dom) and I didn't spend a second dwelling on what happened. I would frequently and firmly shut down any conversations I heard that indulged in speculation about who the perpetrator could be.

In moments of chaos, optimism, proactivity and focus are your friends.

Emotion, despair and pessimism are your enemies.

I knew we wouldn't be able to find out, so it didn't matter, and I didn't want the team to spend even a second of effort on anything other than moving forward.

My natural focus was bringing optimism and confidence back to the team. I had days of individual and collective conversations to rally the troops, to get people fired up, and to let them know that it was my genuine and sincere belief that we were going to come back even stronger than before. Behind the scenes I worked hard to close the investment deal that we had been working on and I decided that myself and Dom wouldn't pay ourselves for the foreseeable future to avoid the need for redundancies.

Business has taught me that there are two types of people in moments of chaos. If a room is burning down, one type of person will stand up, point at the fire and repeatedly scream 'THERE'S A FIRE, OMG THERE IS A FIRE, OMG THERE IS A FIRE. . .' terrifying everyone else in the process. This person will likely go up in flames shortly after. The other type of person won't feel the need to acknowledge the fire; they know that everyone can see and smell it, they know worry isn't useful and they know that every second spent dwelling on the fire is an important second robbed from formulating a plan to get out of the room. They will focus themselves and others on the way out of the room, and their likelihood of survival is tremendously higher. I have naturally always been the latter, and I only promote people to senior leadership roles that demonstrate characteristics of the latter too.

The chaos you find yourself in is nearly always less fatal than it seems in the moment. The only things you can control are your behaviour, emotions and actions – from the moment chaos arrives to the moment it subsides. What has happened has already happened – it's no longer within your control, so do not seek to control it. All you have now are your choices about how to respond and your mindset. Any time spent trying to control the past or anxiously worrying about the future will increase the severity of the situation and reduce your chances of overcoming it. Reminding yourself that you have survived every moment of chaos that life has thrown at you so far, and you're still here now, is a great indicator that you have what it takes to survive this too.

Optimism, proactivity and focus are your friends. Emotion, despair and pessimism are your enemies. If you want to feed a problem, keep thinking about it. If you want to starve a problem, take action.

Over the weeks that followed, the team came together in a remarkably inspiring way – they were optimistic, fired up and aggressively proactive. The energy in the office was electric. I spent the days after the revelations secretly controlling the office playlist to make sure every song was motivating and energising. Myself and Dom paid for special treats for everyone every day and we put extra emphasis on celebrating any win we could. As our sales climbed, and our work continued to improve, it was clear that this episode wasn't going to be fatal after all. A few months later, and largely based on our commercial performance following the hack, we signed that multi-million-pound investment deal securing the future of the company for the years to come.

From the bird's-eye view I had, it's unquestionably clear that the situation would have been fatal for our business if we hadn't reacted appropriately. Optimism, proactivity and focus – without those three things, I wouldn't be here, you wouldn't be reading my book and Social Chain, the $200m social media juggernaut that employees 700+ people around the world, probably wouldn't exist.

That moment was pivotal, and it reaffirmed to me that there is little you can do to stop bad news finding you in life; but when it does find you, the impact it has on you, your future and those you love, will largely be determined by how you react in the moment. Fundamentally we're all the by-product of not what has happened to us, but how we chose to handle it.

You are not what happened to you, you are how you chose to handle it.

Chapter Fourteen

THE EIGHTH WONDER OF THE WORLD

I RECENTLY HIT 1 million followers on Instagram and did one of those corny posts thanking my followers for their support. Don't worry, I didn't do the '1' helium balloon with the glass of champagne, it was just a quick Instagram story thanking my team.

Following my post, I received hundreds of direct messages from other creators and some of my followers asking for tips on growing their Instagram channels in the same way. Whenever I'm asked for tips on how I've achieved something, my brain does what everyone's brain probably does – it rummages around looking for some kind of easy secret hack or cheat to share.

People gravitate towards easy because easy sells much better than complicated and hard – remember the guy asking me for three tips to become a better public speaker? In sales and marketing, if you can create the perception that something 'easy' will yield high returns, it'll sell like hot cakes because we all want small investments to produce large returns.

This is why most click-bait get-rich-quick schemes lead off with headlines like: '6-pack Abs in 7 Minutes' or 'How I Made a Million in 30 Days'. On one end of these sentences you have a big return; on the other end you have a relatively 'easy' investment.

If I was to write an honest click-bait sales headline for success, it would probably read: 'The Simple Thing That Will Make You Successful in 10 Years' Time If You Start Working Hard Now'.

I use the word 'simple' because all of my success was somewhat simple in hindsight. That shouldn't detract from the fact that it was also really really fucking hard.

I don't know if there's a 'secret to success' but I do know that every major achievement I've accomplished has an indisputable simple causal factor in common. The reason I'm currently in the best shape of my life, why I have millions of followers, millions of $$$ in the bank, why I was able to build a global business at 21 years old and the reason why I've managed to persuade you to purchase this book is ultimately because of my consistency over time.

The power of consistency over time is both profound and underrated.

It's profound because it's the most common factor in the story of every 'successful' person I've ever met, but it's underrated because it's totally invisible.

THE EIGHTH WONDER OF THE WORLD

The world's most famous investor is a guy called Warren Buffett. Over his 52-year stint as CEO of Berkshire Hathaway, Buffett has earned a nearly 2 million per cent return on his investors' money. To put that into perspective, if you had invested $10,000 into Berkshire Hathaway in 1965, that investment would be worth $88 million today.

When asked for the single most powerful factor behind his investing success, Warren Buffett responded 'compound interest' without skipping a beat.

BOOKS ×

SELF-HELP RESULTS (910,055)

BE CONSISTENT FOR A LONG TIME

BE CONSISTENT FOR A LONG TIME

BE CONSISTENT FOR A LONG TIME

BE CONSISTENT FOR A LONG TIME

"BE CONSISTENT FOR A LONG TIME"
SHOULD BE THE TITLE OF EVERY SELF-HELP
BOOK EVER WRITTEN.

He's been preaching this for six decades as the key factor that made him a billionaire.

I'm sure you've heard about the power of compounding interest before. In fact, you've probably heard about it many times. What makes this time different? Honestly, nothing. Unless I can persuade you to take it seriously. If I do, I'll quite literally change your entire life forever. The stakes are high. So here goes.

In finance, compound interest simply means that instead of taking out any of the money you've made from your investment, you leave it in and effectively keep earning more interest on your interest. I know this sounds incredibly easy, and therefore like it won't make a big difference, but just like consistency over time, it's ultimately the invisible force that makes all the difference.

Compound interest is such a powerful yet neglected idea that Albert Einstein allegedly called it the 'Eighth Wonder of the World' and said, 'he who understands it, earns it . . . he who doesn't . . . pays it'. If you don't understand it, you're inadvertently paying it.

THE POWER OF COMPOUNDING

Because the power of compounding interest is quite hard to understand in just words, I want to show you a diagram that illustrates it clearly. In this diagram, you have two investors – me and my dog, Pablo. Me and Pablo are having a race to see who can create the most wealth in 30 years' time. Pablo decides to focus on compounding interest by saving his money in an investment account that gives him 15 per cent a year. I don't believe in the power of compounding interest, so I decide I'm going to straight up save $20,000 every year in my piggy bank.

	PABLO		STEVE	
	Investment	Total	Investment	Total
Year 1	$20,000	23,000.00	$20,000	$20,000
Year 2	15% interest	26,450.00	$40,000	$40,000
Year 3	15% interest	29,900.00	$60,000	$60,000
Year 4	15% interest	34,385.00	$80,000	$80,000
Year 5	15% interest	39,542.75	$100,000	$100,000
Year 6	15% interest	45,474.16	$120,000	$120,000
Year 7	15% interest	52,295.29	$140,000	$140,000
Year 8	15% interest	60,139.58	$160,000	$160,000
Year 9	15% interest	69,160.52	$180,000	$180,000
Year 10	15% interest	79,534.59	$200,000	$200,000
Year 11	15% interest	91,464.78	$220,000	$220,000
Year 12	15% interest	105,184.50	$240,000	$240,000
Year 13	15% interest	120,962.18	$260,000	$260,000
Year 14	15% interest	139,106.50	$280,000	$280,000
Year 15	15% interest	159,972.48	$300,000	$300,000
Year 16	15% interest	183,968.35	$320,000	$320,000
Year 17	15% interest	211,563.60	$340,000	$340,000
Year 18	15% interest	243,298.14	$360,000	$360,000
Year 19	15% interest	279,792.86	$380,000	$380,000
Year 20	15% interest	321,761.79	$400,000	$400,000
Year 21	15% interest	370,026.06	$420,000	$420,000
Year 22	15% interest	425,529.97	$440,000	$440,000
Year 23	15% interest	489,359.47	$460,000	$460,000
Year 24	15% interest	562,763.39	$480,000	$480,000
Year 25	15% interest	647,177.90	$500,000	$500,000
Year 26	15% interest	744,254.58	$520,000	$520,000
Year 27	15% interest	855,892.77	$540,000	$540,000
Year 28	15% interest	984,276.68	$560,000	$560,000
Year 29	15% interest	1,131,918.19	$580,000	$580,000
Year 30	15% interest	1,301,705.91	$600,000	$600,000

In 30 years' time, although Pablo only ever saved $20,000, he's now a millionaire. And although I put 30x more than him into my piggy bank ($600,000) I'm not. The interest Pablo accrued on his money gave his investment some kind of invisible momentum that mine didn't have.

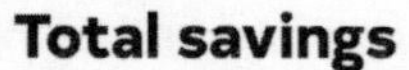

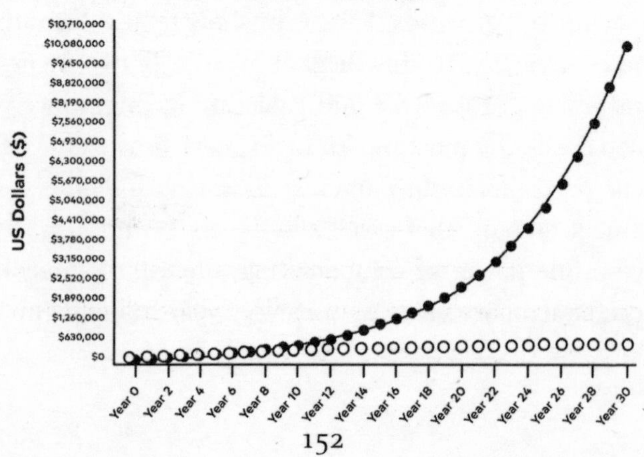

That invisible momentum is what Albert Einstein was referring to as the Eighth Wonder of the World: compounding interest.

THE POWER OF TIME

Clearly furious and confused, imagine that I reverse time and ask Pablo for a rematch. He humbly agrees. This time, Pablo tells me that he's going to invest $20,000 every year from year 1 until year 10, into his compounding interest account with a 15 per cent interest rate. Upon hearing this, and keen to beat him, I decide to invest for double the time, in the same compound interest account, but I decide to start investing from year 10 until year 30. Here's what happens.

	PABLO		STEVE	
	Investment	Total	Investment	Total
Year 1	$20,000	23,000.00		
Year 2	$20,000	49,450.00		
Year 3	$20,000	79,867.50		
Year 4	$20,000	114,847.63		
Year 5	$20,000	155,074.77		
Year 6	$20,000	201,335.98		
Year 7	$20,000	254,536.38		
Year 8	$20,000	315,716.84		
Year 9	$20,000	386,074.36		
Year 10	$20,000	466,985.52	$20,000	23,000.00
Year 11		537,033.35	$20,000	49,450.00
Year 12		617,588.35	$20,000	79,876.50
Year 13		710,226.60	$20,000	114,847.63
Year 14		816,760.59	$20,000	155,074.77
Year 15		939,274.68	$20,000	201,335.98
Year 16		1,080,165.88	$20,000	254,536.38
Year 17		1,242,190.77	$20,000	315,716.84
Year 18		1,428,519.38	$20,000	386,074.36
Year 19		1,642,797.29	$20,000	466,985.52
Year 20		1,889,216.88	$20,000	560,033.35
Year 21		2,172,599.41	$20,000	667,038.35
Year 22		2,498,489.32	$20,000	790,094.10
Year 23		2,873,262.72	$20,000	931,608.22
Year 24		3,304,252.13	$20,000	1,094,349.45
Year 25		3,799,889.95	$20,000	1,281,501.87
Year 26		4,369,873.44	$20,000	1,496,727.15
Year 27		5,025,354.46	$20,000	1,744,236.22
Year 28		5,779,157.63	$20,000	2,028,871.65
Year 29		6,646,031.28	$20,000	2,356,202.40
Year 30		7,642,935.97	$20,000	2,732,632.76

To my horror, 30 years later, despite the fact that I've invested $20,000 for 10 more years than Pablo, Pablo still ends up with almost $5,000,000 more than me! And therein lies a key factor of compounding efforts and consistency – time. In the context of your career, finances, business and fitness goals, the sooner you get started, the sooner you begin investing, learning, building experience and therefore creating this invisible momentum, the better. Time is everything. Starting as soon as possible and being consistent is the magic to unlocking the invisible but defining rewards of compounding interest, compounding efforts and compounding success.

Gary Keller and Jay Papasan, authors of *The ONE Thing*, explain how focusing on compounding momentum can bring the same invisible and magical returns that we see in these finance examples to all areas of your life. They say: 'Where I had huge success, I had narrowed my concentration to one thing, and where my success varied, my focus had too. Success is sequential, not simultaneous.' The phrase 'success is sequential' speaks to the important role every daily decision and ounce of effort ultimately plays in your eventual success.

My 1-million-follower milestone is the perfect example of sequential success, consistency over time and how every post mattered – even the posts from when I had 100 followers. Ultimately, my growth was compounding from day 1, that first post took me from 100 followers to 101 followers, those 101 followers are the reason I got to 102 followers and so on. It was a consistent chain of effort, growth, learning and progress that gradually gained momentum over the course of five years.

Astonishingly, the first 800 posts I did got me to 10,000 followers. The next 800 posts added an additional 1 million followers. If you look at this on a graph, it's identical to the exponential growth we see in Pablo's investment when he benefited from 15 per cent compounding interest.

SUCCESS:

5% BRAINS

95% CONSISTENCY

Consistency compounds in the same way. You just can't see it while it's happening and compounding is slow then sudden.

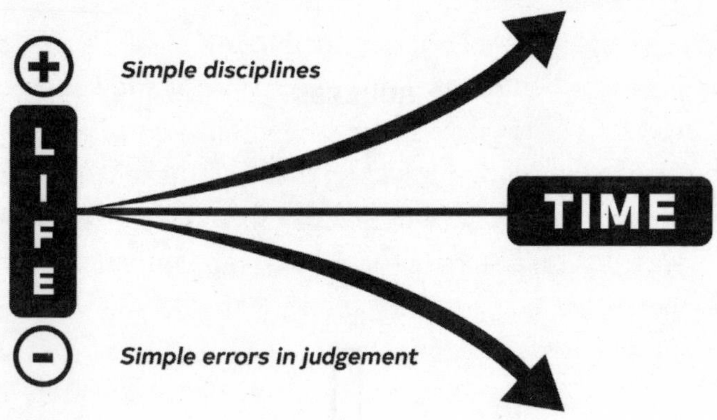

INVISIBLE PR

The Eighth Wonder of the World isn't just working for or against your bank balance, it's at work slowly, and virtually invisibly, shifting the trajectory of every aspect of your life: your health, your mental health, your reputation, your relationships – everything. I saw this most clearly as the CEO of Social Chain. I saw how a series of small, seemingly insignificant decisions that team members made gently furthered their reputation, trustworthiness and eligibility for promotion, or how small and seemingly insignificant decisions did the opposite.

Your reputation is a series of persuasive stories that live in other people's minds. Those 'other people' use those stories to make key decisions about you; to choose how to treat you and to decide how to interact with you. You can't and you shouldn't live your life solely trying to improve the perception other people have of you in their minds – that's a path destined for misery. That's also not what matters as it relates to reputation

– reputation cares more about your fundamentals, your integrity, trustworthiness, morals, how you treat other people and how accountable you are to your word.

I remember being sat in our New York office and getting a text from a team member in our London office telling me that Steph in Design had jumped up from her desk and run to the shops to get a plaster for a colleague who had cut their finger without being asked. Steph had no idea that I even knew this – I was 5,500 miles away – but that one seemingly insignificant action was the first story written into her reputation in my mind, and a story that stayed front of mind when we discussed her promotion several months later.

As the CEO of more than 700 team members, and from the bird's-eye view it gave me, I witnessed how these tiny actions were compounding for or against everyone in the company. Team members that excelled in sales and with 'natural talent' were unable to progress at the rate they should have because of innocuous actions that had created blemishes to their reputation. It wasn't the few big, positive actions that were determining their progress, it was the seemingly insignificant negative stories.

After several years of being in the room when directors discussed team promotions, this became so patently obvious to me that I branded it 'Invisible PR'. Every time a new member joined the team, and I had a chance to speak to them, I would tell them about this powerful, intangible force that would determine their success here and throughout their life. I told them that they would never get to see their Invisible PR, they wouldn't even know when they were adding to it positively or negatively, but I assured them that it would show up when it mattered the most to their progression.

You, me and everyone else reading this book has their own

Invisible PR which is compounding for or against them right now. It's built on every action and decision you make. It isn't necessarily accurate, and it isn't always true, but as it relates to Invisible PR, then truth doesn't matter and perception is considered reality. At all times, with everything you do or don't do, you're incrementally adding positively or negatively to yours. Over the span of a decade or the course of a lifetime, your Invisible PR will have more influence over the trajectory and direction of your life than any other force. This is because, in the world we live in, every barrier or path to progress is guarded by other people. The only thing standing in the way of you becoming the leader of your country, the best salesperson in the world, a world-leading philanthropist or the CEO of a global company is a bunch of people.

Focus neurotically on the small stuff. Value your integrity, trustworthiness, your morals, how you treat other people and your word obsessively. Protect your Invisible PR like your life depends on it – because it does.

MY DENTIST WAS A PHILOSOPHER

When I was 14, I bragged to my dentist that my teeth were perfect despite how infrequently I had brushed them. The fact that I was the only 14-year-old I knew without fillings, cavities or any dental ailment had given me a 'dental arrogance' which, of course, I later regretted. Dennis the Dentist, as I called him, said something to me that I've never forgotten.

'Steven,' he said. 'If you don't brush your teeth today, your teeth will be fine. If you don't brush your teeth tomorrow, your teeth will be fine. But if you don't brush your teeth every day for the next five years, in five years' time, you're going to be sitting here screaming as I pull and drill all the rotten ones out.' I laughed nervously, left his practice and I don't recall ever going back.

It took me 10 years to really understand and embrace what he meant. What Dennis the Dentist was telling me was that this 'invisible momentum' can also work against you – especially if you're arrogant enough to believe it won't. In the same way, today's hard work and focus won't produce great results today, tomorrow's hard work and focus won't produce great returns tomorrow, but hard work for 10 years will create an invisible force of momentum so strong that it can carve through mountains. Literally. In the case of the Grand Canyon, which is considered one of the seven natural wonders of the world, its 2,000-metre awe-inspiring depth was carved by nothing more than very consistent water over a long period of time.

If you spent 10 days dumping billions of gallons of water on a mountain, the water would ultimately have no lasting impact. But if you spend millions of years pouring a little bit of water on a mountain, consistency and time will change the shape of the mountain indefinitely.

Similarly, people tend to believe that the key to success lies in short bursts of intensity (7-day diets, get-rich-quick schemes, a two-week meditation retreat). This is the equivalent of dumping billions of gallons of water on a mountain and expecting a grand canyon. The answer, as James Clear, author of *Atomic Habits,* often points out is consistency: 'Most people need consistency more than they need intensity. Intensity makes a good story. Consistency makes progress.' Instead of a crash diet, make a small change to your diet that you can maintain for the next year; instead of get-rich-quick schemes, read a few pages of the best business books every day; instead of a meditation retreat, meditate for 10 minutes a day every day. That's how you'll fundamentally change the shape of your life.

Success is the result of your consistency invisibly compounding for or against you, over long periods of time.

The reason people don't do the small things that ultimately add up to success is because, at first, the small things don't add up to success. In fact, we never really see small decisions significantly benefit us or significantly cost us in the moment, so we don't value them.

And if you don't value them, I don't blame you; surely it's insanity to continually do something that apparently has no visible impact. In fact, there's a famous misattributed Albert Einstein quote that says, 'Insanity is doing the same thing over and over again and expecting different results.' So surely all of those aspiring bodybuilders lifting those iron dumbbells up and down are crazy?

If you make the correct small decisions today for your physical health, mental health, career, finances, business or relationships, you won't see the results today. Success is the result of your consistency invisibly compounding for you, over long periods of time.

You have to want your success enough and enjoy the process enough to be willing to believe in and work for it, potentially for years, without actually being able to see it compounding.

By the time your success arrives, the world acknowledges your results, applauds you, puts you on the Forbes list, buys your book and follows you on Instagram, those small, correct decisions that put you in that position will be ancient history, and the results of the small decisions you made today will still be invisible.

According to the University of Scranton, almost 92 per cent of people never actually achieve their goals. If everyone truly believed in the power of their consistency compounding over time, I'm convinced that statistic would be reversed. Our small decisions are grossly underestimated, and our big decisions are typically overestimated.

There's this misleading narrative that greatness is a singular decision – one race, a choice, one heroic act, one defining moment or Olympic world record. It's a narrative I spent the first two decades of my life believing. Upon achieving my own success, I realised how wrong, misleading and unhelpful that idea was. My success wasn't the result of one great act; it was the result of many small, good acts, repeated over 10 years. Greatness isn't one decision. Great is just good repeated, over and over again.

GREATNESS ISN'T ONE
BIG DECISION,

GREATNESS IS JUST
GOOD REPEATED.

Chapter Fifteen

MY ASSISTANT CAN'T TALK TO ME ON MONDAYS

MY ASSISTANT, SOPHIE, is a lot more than just my assistant. She's also one of my best friends and a close, trusted confidante. We talk about anything and everything together. She'll tell me about her personal life, her family, her problems and her relationships (or lack thereof). There is, however, one thing she's banned from talking to me about: the gym.

That may sound harsh, and I would prefer if you didn't think I'm an arsehole, so please give me a chance to explain. For the last four years, Sophie has announced to me every single week, and sometimes multiple times a week, that she feels unhealthy so she's going to start going to the gym and she's going to stop eating the foods that make her feel awful. She tells me why she's going to do it, the day she's going to start and the preparations she's made ahead of her new goal. However, she hasn't done it, despite hundreds of these predictable announcements.

At first, I was relatively forgiving and didn't pay much attention to it, but after a year of the same Monday morning announcement, followed by the inevitable explanation as to why it 'wasn't possible' this week, I decided that maybe there was something I could do to help. The fact that she announced this goal once a week did indicate that it mattered to her, and so in an attempt to be a good friend, I offered to pay for her to get a personal trainer as many times each week as she wanted to.

Unfortunately, that didn't work either. She didn't organise the PT session and so she didn't go. Ten more Monday morning announcements later, and increasingly sick of her lack of follow-through, I decided that I would hire a PT on her behalf and I would take her to the gym next to our office after work and we would work out with her. Despite publicly announcing to myself and everyone within earshot that she was going to go and that she thought this was a great idea, I had to figuratively drag her there kicking and screaming. On the first day she actually tried to offer me a small cash bribe while we were stood outside the gym to buy her way out of going inside. This theatrical performance played out for three days straight. On the fourth day, I was stuck in London on business meetings so I told her to head to the gym on her own and meet the PT there.

You can probably guess what transpired . . . She didn't go and that marked the end of Sophie's gym/health and fitness career. Regrettably, it didn't mark the end of her announcing to me and the team that sit near us every Monday that she was going to start going to the gym.

Sophie isn't unique. We all have friends like this and we all act like this at times. As I mentioned in the previous chapter, research shows that almost 92 per cent of people never actually achieve their goals. When I've asked Sophie why she hasn't managed to follow through on her commitment for four years she's said things to me like 'I'm just exhausted today, I'll go next week', or 'I'm so tired' *yawns in your face to prove it* or she admits to not having the 'willpower' on that particular day because of how demanding her schedule is.

I spent the last chapter talking about the tremendous importance of doing the small stuff right and doing it right consistently. The problem is, things that are easy to do are also easy not to do. It's easy to spend two minutes brushing your teeth, so it's also easy not to. It's easy to save $5 once a week, so it's also easy not to. It's easy to do a 20-minute workout at home, so it's also easy not to. This simple truth, added to the fact that the rewards of doing the small stuff are invisible in the moment, makes it incredibly easy to be inconsistent with the all-important small stuff.

When we set out to achieve a big, long-term goal like Sophie but we can't manage to find the discipline to do the small, short-term stuff – like going to the gym – we tend to tell ourselves that it's because we're 'tired', 'unmotivated' or lacking 'willpower'. This is just another false, lazy, unhelpful, over-simplistic, self-fulfilling, binary box that we voluntarily jump inside in an attempt to explain a complex issue with a simple binary solution.

What did I tell you about avoiding binary boxes?

THE SCIENCE SAYS YOU'RE LIMITING YOURSELF

The reason I refer to this as self-fulfilling is because all the reliable science on the matter suggests that it is. Beginning in the early 2000s, research began to emerge suggesting that willpower depletion only exists for those who believe their willpower is depleting. That means, only those who believe their willpower is diminished will experience diminished willpower. You become what you tell yourself you are.

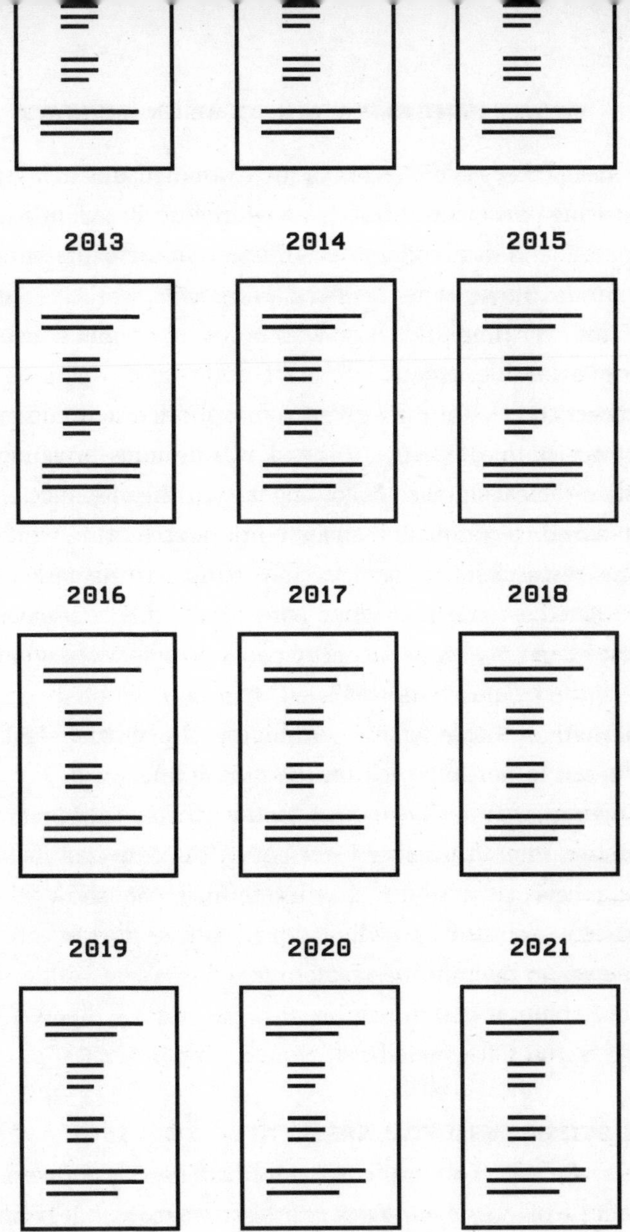

WE'RE ALL ACTORS, UNCONSCIOUSLY ACTING OUT THE STORIES WE TOLD OURSELVES ABOUT OURSELVES, LONG AGO.

A researcher called Veronika Job examined this idea by first measuring participants' beliefs on willpower. Based on a survey, Veronika and her colleagues grouped participants into two categories: those who believed willpower was limited and depletes over time, and those who believed willpower is unlimited and doesn't deplete.

Participants were then given a complicated and demanding writing task to complete – this task was designed to potentially 'deplete' their willpower. Following the writing task, participants were asked to complete a challenging puzzle.

The researchers found that the tiring writing task caused diminished performance when participants then worked on the puzzle – but only for those participants who believed willpower was limited. Those who believed it to be unlimited were not exhausted or depleted by completing the writing task and continued to perform well on the puzzle afterward.

This research has been replicated with consistent outcomes by many other researchers subsequently. Many psychologists now believe, as a result, that individuals can show extreme levels of self-control and willpower, so long as they believe their willpower to be a limitless resource.

So, Sophie, if you're reading this, it's not a willpower issue – unless you tell yourself it is.

YOU DECIDE WHO YOU ARE

Labels are the short-cut, over-simplified descriptions we give ourselves, of ourselves. They are binary boxes that contain a series of implicit instructions on who you are and how you should behave. People take on labels that they've foolishly given themselves in an attempt to make themselves make sense, to make themselves understood and often to make themselves matter: parent, girlfriend, boss, rich, poor, tall, old, young, ditsy, lazy, unmotivated, creative, procrastinator, forgetful, thick, smart, entrepreneur, athlete, marketeer, builder, mum, dad.

What is it you tell yourself you are? Isn't it funny that your life continues to follow that exact storyline? You know that's not a coincidence, don't you?

Once you're inside a labelled box, the science says you'll naturally start acting like the label written on the front of the box; the longer you conform to the stereotype of your label, the harder it becomes to ever become anything but that label. Therefore, the box you've put yourself in, and the label associated with it, can be the making or breaking of you. Either way, it's likely to limit you.

I spent the last decade building one of the world's most successful social media marketing companies but I promise you, as tempting as it might be, I do not allow myself to consider myself a 'CEO', a 'marketeer' or a 'social media expert'. I'm just a fucking guy that applied my skills to one particular challenge, at one point, and learned a little more about that challenge every day. I will not label myself, because for all its convenience, I know how limiting labels can become.

Applying myself to a challenge and being successful in doing so does not make me that challenge. I'm just a human with a bunch of skills, experience and perspectives that I apply to challenges that I believe to be worthwhile – I'm not my job, my past accomplishments, marital status, my future ambitions, a headline or my speaker bio. This year I've organised a theatrical show that I'm producing, acoustically editing and directing – we sold all 900 tickets in the first three minutes. I'm also working on an unorthodox solution to some of the world's most crippling mental health challenges; I'm taking on the broken, outdated and deceptive university education system; I'm producing the third series of my own chart-topping podcast;

I'm creating an app for time management and also . . . of course. . . I'm writing a book. Oh, I'm also the dad to a French Bulldog called Pablo – that very financially savvy little pup.

There's a term in sociology called 'labelling theory', and it states that people come to identify and behave in ways that reflect how others label them – they become the labels they're given. This theory is often associated with the sociology of crime since it's been proven that labelling someone unlawfully deviant can lead to them becoming unlawfully deviant – that means if everyone starts calling you and treating you like a criminal, that alone can increase the chances of you acting like one.

I would go as far as saying, there is no force in the world that has greater positive or negative influence over you, your potential and your future than the series of stubborn labels you've given yourself, or accepted, and the often irrational stories that inspired them.

It takes a great deal of fresh, believable evidence to remove your negative labels and to replace them with more constructive, healthy ones – but the good news is, it is possible. When I was 18 years old, I met a 26-year-old guy at a hip-hop event in Manchester – he was short, inaudible, lacking in confidence and dressed head to toe in an awful white tracksuit.

His name was Ashley and, unbeknown to me, he was unemployed, living off jobseeker's allowance and passing his time playing video games at his mum's house where he lived. A few weeks after that event, after finding out that I was running my own company, Ashley messaged me on Facebook asking if he could work for me. Busy, and inundated with messages, I ignored him. Undeterred, and unwilling to take my ghosting as an answer, Ashley messaged me again.

Ashley was unqualified and inexperienced but, unfortunately, so was I, and that probably explains why I offered him the job as marketing director without so much as an interview.

He spent the next six years working next to me, in our founding team, building what would become one of the most formidable businesses in our industry. As I write this today, here in the jungle in Costa Rica, Ashley is the 33-year-old CEO and founder of his own company and that company is leading the way within its industry. That short, inaudible, seemingly introverted guy that I met six years ago appears to have grown an extra foot in height, has become the most self-assured voice in the room and set fire to all the labelled boxes he once called home.

I didn't know anything about Ash's circumstances, so I didn't treat him like his circumstances. In finding the confidence to repeatedly message me, it would appear that Ash also disregarded the labels commonly associated with his circumstances. Because he was able to reject the temptation to become his circumstances, Ash was able to create an opportunity, which allowed him to build the self-belief and evidence he needed to adopt a new set of labels and to ultimately establish wildly better circumstances.

Self-belief is a grossly misunderstood concept. For some bizarre reason, the most common advice given to people lacking in self-belief seems to be . . . 'just believe in yourself'. These words are plastered across motivational Instagram accounts, posters, gym walls and self-help books, as if just uttering them will change the deep-rooted and hardwired beliefs we have of ourselves and our capabilities, as if our belief system were as mouldable as plasticine.

Your beliefs about yourself are the by-product of years of conditioning, childhood experiences, decades of consuming media stereotypes and hundreds of thousands of hours of feedback from friends, family and total strangers. Sadly it's going to take more than a motivational quote on Instagram or a few well-meaning words of encouragement from a friend to uproot them.

But understanding that – understanding how stubborn they are – is the first step in being able to do something about them.

That's because we don't get to decide what we believe. Even if we really want to believe something, even if everything that matters to us depended on us adopting that belief, we couldn't. Our beliefs are the by-product of the subjective evidence we have and our own interpretations of that evidence.

If you want to uproot them, words alone aren't enough; you have to expose yourself to new evidence that challenges them, that contradicts them and that categorically disproves them.

My friend Ashley is a prime example – the tumultuous, wild ride we went on building a global business together taught us both what we were truly capable of. It stretched our horizons and expanded our self-belief and once you see what you're capable of, you can't simply unsee it – our positive beliefs are terribly stubborn too. If I rewound time by six years, and I turned to Ashley at that first event and said, 'You're more than capable of being the CEO of your own successful company,' it would have washed over him like rain off an umbrella – like telling someone to 'just believe in yourself'.

YOU DON'T WANT IT, YOU JUST WANT TO WANT IT

Going back to my assistant, Sophie, for a second, the reason she can't seem to do what she wants to do isn't just because of the 'limited willpower fallacy' she's bought into or because of a label she's given herself; it's also because of a series of psychological barriers that are subconsciously undermining her.

I sat down with world-renowned author Nir Eyal to discuss this further. His most recent research, and his latest book,

Indistractable, endeavour to uncover why we often can't seem to do the things we say we want to. Nir told me:

> "People wrongly assume that we make our decisions based on pleasure and comfort, but this is fundamentally not the case; our decisions are innately driven by our desire to avoid discomfort. The same internal response we have to physical discomfort applies to our psychological discomfort too, so when we feel uncomfortable emotions like fear, boredom, and loneliness we have all kinds of solutions we turn to in order to make these uncomfortable sensations in our heads go away, to avoid them, from procrastination, excuses or distraction. We're never going to stop becoming distracted from our goals if we don't fundamentally understand what discomfort we're trying to escape from and what's causing it."

In Sophie's case, she's repeatedly vented that she doesn't know what she's doing at the gym, that she's concerned with how she looks while she's working out and about who might see her there looking hot and bothered. On the three days that she begrudgingly worked out with me and a PT, she spent most of the time looking over her shoulder and apologising for how 'weak' and 'unfit' she was. This is when I realised that Nir was right. As much as Sophie does want to be the type of person that goes to the gym, and as much as she wants to achieve the results that the gym has to offer, there are a series of deep-rooted issues around going to the gym that are creating seemingly insurmountable psychological discomfort for her, and these issues relate to her self-esteem and her self-confidence.

There is no self-development without self-awareness. You can read as many books as you like, but if you're unable to read yourself, you'll never learn a thing.

Remember Ashley and the self-belief and the effort it takes to re-label ourselves? So just telling Sophie to go to the gym isn't going to work – her limiting beliefs and self-esteem issues are evidently too stubborn and embedded to be overcome with a few words of encouragement. She tactically circumvents and evades scenarios that bring her psychological discomfort by making irrational excuses and future-facing promises to address it next week – which turns into the week after, and then the week after and then the week after.

Sophie doesn't actually want to go to the gym; our choices generally represent what we really want to do. In her subconscious mind the gym is the root cause of psychological discomfort – but she wishes she wanted to go. This is the difference between her vocal intentions and her ultimate actions. Unfortunately, intention is nothing without action and action is nothing without intention. Progress happens when your intentions and actions become the same thing. She has to want to go to the gym.

Many of us have this inability to go to the gym, largely the effect of a much deeper unaddressed self-esteem issue. We all live our lives blind to the root cause of our behaviours, but it's these behaviours that determine who we actually become, not who we say we want to become. You'll do what you want to do, not what you want to want to do.

I spent a few years mentoring a guy who wanted to become a business leader, yet every time he was placed in a senior management role he became an authoritarian dictator, bossing people around, micro-managing them and seemingly insistent on making sure everyone knew his job title, accomplishments and superiority. He wasn't a bad guy – in fact, he was one of the nicest, gentlest and most caring people I've met – and when I spoke to him he was able to identify that his behaviour wasn't productive. Just like Sophie, he verbally pledged to rectify it, to make a change and to be different in the future – but just like Sophie, he couldn't, which ultimately led to him losing his dream job.

You don't need a degree in psychology to understand that there was some kind of insecurity driving his behaviour. A few years earlier, during one of our conversations, he recalled a moment when he was a child that he's never forgotten. One day, his mother, who was his only parent due to a tragedy with his father, had left the house and totally forgotten that she hadn't taken him with her. Upon her return, she looked down and jokingly said, 'I totally forgot about you.' He confessed to me that since that unforgettable day, he's always had a burning desire to prove to everyone that he's 'enough'. Some 30 years later those words, and the story they made him believe about himself, are still negatively influencing his behaviour. There's a horrible paradox in the fact that his own belief that he's not enough caused a behaviour pattern that is now stopping him from becoming all that he could be.

Motivational words and positive intentions stand no chance against our psychological hard wiring. No matter what motivational seminar, talk or course you attend, you'll quickly return to your default psychological state if that motivational talk doesn't inspire you to take action that ultimately leads you to create new evidence about who you are and what you're capable of.

We waste so much time and energy trying to justify the adverse effects of deep-rooted issues with surface-level answers. This is why I believe that one of the most valuable things you can do, for your mental health and your future, is to journal or keep a diary. It's impossibly difficult for most of us to understand why we do the things we do just by thinking about it.

The forces driving us are instinctive, deep and subconscious. However, all of my most valuable personal life-changing revelations and discoveries have come from talking to my diary, critically analysing my behaviour from an overview and the deep introspection that journaling inspires.

Those subconscious forces inside you will overpower the best advice in the world, your 'reasonable pilot', new information, this book and pretty much anything your best friend tells you. You can read as many books as you like, but if you can't read yourself, you'll never learn a thing.

Therapy, and the benefit of having a truly objective sounding board, can inspire even more valuable insights. If you're doing neither and you're just 'going with the flow', it will be difficult for you to ever truly overcome your most limiting beliefs.

We're all actors, unconsciously acting out the stories we told ourselves about ourselves long ago. If there is a single force in this world that is holding you back, it probably isn't other people, your boss, the political party in charge or even your circumstances; it is you, and the stories you believe about you.

I USED TO RUN AWAY FROM GIRLS I LOVED

At 15 years old, I had my 'first love': that beautiful playground goddess called Jasmine. My pursuit of Jasmine lasted for almost four years. It was one of those irrational, adolescent, spellbinding first loves – she occupied my mind, drove my decisions and inspired the playlist on my MP3 player for much of that time.

Adding to the complexity of the situation was the fact that Jasmine had a long-term boyfriend at another school. Needless to say, I hated his guts and he hated mine. We came close to physical warfare on several occasions around town, at parties and wherever else our paths crossed. Undeterred and unwilling to let that stand in the way of my unrelenting love for her, I pursued her doggedly. By 16 years old, I had made great progress. She clearly liked me and she had clearly figured out that he was a d*ckhead. We would sneak a little kiss once in a while, we held hands in school and she had agreed to be my prom date!

A week after prom, the day I had fought for for years finally arrived. One day, after school, me and Jasmine met up behind the school gates. We stood hand in hand, she looked me in the eyes and told me, 'I'm going to end things with Joe, then we can be together . . .'

Suddenly, and unexpectedly, this feeling of terror, regret and fear consumed me. 'Ah, fuck no!' I heard a panicked murmur in my mind.

'I don't think that's a good idea, Jasmine,' I replied.

'I don't think you should do that,' I continued.

I quickly changed the subject, gave her a kiss and made my exit.

This sounds like absolute insanity now, but at the time it didn't. I was just acting on what I felt. I wasn't conscious of my behaviour and its causes; I wasn't aware of the powerful subconscious forces that drive all of us in the shadows, and I was too young to really understand myself.

I spent years relentlessly pursuing a girl and the minute she told me she would be with me, I panicked and rejected her. I wish I could tell you that Jasmine was the first and last time this happened – but she wasn't. This bizarre pattern repeated itself time and time again until I was 23 years old. That's the reason I wrote 'Hold a long-term relationship' in my diary as one of my four goals to achieve before I was 25.

Just like Sophie and the gym, I had the intention to be Jasmine's boyfriend but when I had the opportunity to realise that intention, some overpowering subconscious force stood in my way. It took me 10 years to understand that force, to confront it and then to overcome it.

I told you in Chapter 1 that my mother is a flamboyant, passionate African woman. However, I think that's probably an understatement. When I was a kid, she had a passion for volume, shouting and chaos. I spent most of my childhood watching her screaming at my passive English father. I recall her standing in front of Dad while he tried to watch his favourite show and shouting at him at a volume so excruciatingly loud it left my eardrums ringing afterwards. I remember her chasing him through our house with a knife and him calling the police. I remember her stood screaming in the middle of the street because she was unhappy with him. And I remember her being locked up for public disorder.

My mum's bouts of chaos would last for hours on end. I couldn't quite believe that one person could scream and shout for five to six hours without pause, and on many occasions I would try to intervene in a bid to pacify – but I don't recall that ever working. When I was still quite young, my dad called me into his bedroom and told me that they didn't love each other and a few years later he told me at the kitchen table that they were going to get a divorce. They never did get that divorce, but the chaos, mayhem and stress left a lasting mark on me that I would struggle to heal for the best part of a decade. Psychologists agree on the profound influence that early experiences have on us in later life, they also agree that key authority figures, like our parents, have a disproportionate impact on our belief system.

Without realising it, the relationship our parents have with each other often becomes the first and most important model we learn from for what love, romance and intimacy are. Without realising it, my parents had taught me that relationships were a negative thing. I had learned that being with a woman will hold you back, stress you out and make you miserable. They taught me that love was an inescapable prison sentence, and subconsciously, deep down in the depths of my programming, I believed that if I ever got into a relationship I too would become miserable, trapped and stressed.

This explains the feelings of dread, anxiety and fear that consumed me when Jasmine finally gave me a chance. As Nir Eyal said, we'll never achieve our goals 'if we don't fundamentally understand what psychological discomfort we're trying to escape from'. Had I not had this realisation and connected the dots, there's a high chance I would never have experienced the unmatched fulfilment of romantic love that a full relationship can give you.

Self-help gurus will often preach that growth is achieved by learning new things, but the truth is, growth is achieved by learning *and* unlearning at the same time. Reading books like this is a great way to learn. Reading yourself is a great way to *unlearn*. If you can do both, you can make progress. If you just do one, you'll fail.

By 23 years old, I had understood, confronted and largely overcome this subconscious conditioning. That year, I found love again and had my first long-term romantic relationship. You'll probably notice that I said 'largely overcome'. The truth is that childhood conditioning can be so stubborn, persistent and powerful that you may struggle to ever fully overcome it.

READING BOOKS IS A GREAT WAY TO LEARN.
READING YOURSELF IS A GREAT WAY TO UNLEARN.

IF YOU DO BOTH, YOU'LL MOVE FORWARD.
IF YOU DO ONE, YOU'LL GO ROUND IN CIRCLES.

For example, whenever I have a disagreement with a romantic partner today, I still completely refuse to allow it to become a heated argument. I simply will not do it. I'm happy to have a conversation or a respectful argument, but the minute things get heated, antagonistic or aggressive, I will either refuse to engage or I'll get my things and leave. This might sound like an admirable quality in a boyfriend, but my ex-partners tend to disagree – when you're shouting at your boyfriend and he goes completely silent or walks away, I'm told it can be extremely frustrating.

For me, unpicking the stories I believed about romantic relationships, being emotionally aware of how they influenced me and noting when that influence rears its ugly head has been enough to weaken its power over me and prevent it from getting in the way of my happy romantic relationships.

Without a shadow of a doubt, there will be a thousand more stories that I've learned about myself, the world and the way it works that are both untrue and fundamentally holding me back from being even more fulfilled, being a better romantic partner and reaching higher success. The same applies for you. I can't tell you what those stories are in your life, but if your intentions don't seem to match your actions and outcomes, that's probably a good place to look.

HERE'S WHY I'LL GO BROKE

Most of the pain, embarrassment and shame of my childhood can be directly linked back to my family's relative poverty when I was aged between 10 and 18 years old. I was at the age where I felt terribly ashamed to pull up at school in a battered old van, to live in a derelict house and to not have the same 'things' as the other kids.

Everyone buys books, few ever read them. Everyone wants growth, few accept pain. Everyone wants to be happier, few ever change.

Intention is nothing without action, but action is nothing without intention.

Progress happens when your intentions and actions become the same thing.

I hated watching my mum and dad argue about money, and I couldn't understand why we didn't get presents on Christmas and birthdays.

This evidently left a mark on me that would develop into a subconscious insecurity. It's most certainly the reason why my brothers and I all vowed to become millionaires and most certainly why I've spent so much of my life caring about overt displays of wealth.

At 21 years old, when I first started earning serious money, I would spend over £50,000 a year just on Dom Perignon champagne in nightclubs. I spent tens of thousands on Louis Vuitton. I bought that Range Rover Sport I wrote about at 18 years old in my diary and I rented that beautiful six-bedroom mansion complete with everything.

What a stupid, insecure, attention-seeking idiot I was.

Just like my gym-avoiding assistant, Sophie, or my bizarre 15-year-old Jasmine-obsessive self, there were unaddressed subconscious forces calling the shots in the background. We are creatures that seek positive reinforcement and the overt displays of wealth made me feel good, so I simply did it more often. I didn't pause to ask myself why spending hundreds of thousands of pounds on things I didn't need to impress other people was making me feel so good. I didn't see the threat this behaviour posed and, to be honest, I couldn't seem to stop anyway.

People tend to believe that money can turn a good person into a bad person – this is untrue. Money doesn't corrupt you; it just gives the subconscious forces that run your life in the background more resources to play with, and that can be a dangerous thing depending on what happened to you in your past and what it led you to believe.

As I've said, we love to think we're in control of ourselves, but we're often not. We're largely driven by good and bad narratives, stories and experiences from our past. You don't know why you do what you do most of the time – you just do it. Often the things that invalidated you when you were a child will be the things you seek validation from as an adult.

It took me three years to uncover, admit and consciously confront the unhelpful stories about money, status and self-esteem that were driving my irresponsible spending habits. Because these insecurities are now conscious – like the fears I held about romantic relationships – they are manageable and relatively powerless. So much unhappiness comes from trying to make other people believe we're happy or significant. It turns out that validation is an inside job – only *you* can validate you.

THE MOST CONVINCING SIGN THAT SOMEONE IS TRULY LIVING THEIR BEST LIFE, IS THEIR LACK OF DESIRE TO SHOW THE WORLD THAT THEY'RE LIVING THEIR BEST LIFE.

YOUR BEST LIFE WON'T SEEK VALIDATION.

Chapter Sixteen

HOW TO TAKE RESPONSIBILITY LIKE A HAPPY SEXY MILLIONAIRE IF YOU'RE UNHAPPY, UGLY AND BROKE

'. . . THEY'VE PISSED me off because they haven't paid my invoice,' raged my content executive, Adam, as he forcefully threw his bag to the floor and sank into his chair in a petulant sulk. It was the end of the month, and one of his clients in New York hadn't paid their invoice on time for the third consecutive month. He spent the rest of the day in a stubborn, foul, depressive mood, repeatedly pronouncing 'a client's pissed me off by not paying my invoice on time' like a broken record, whenever someone asked him why he was visibly dismayed.

This sentence structure, 'X made me Y because of Z', is one we're all familiar with. We all say it, hear it and understand it. I think it's important to understand that any time you use this sentence structure, you're lying to yourself and doing yourself a huge disservice at the same time. This sentence mitigates all the responsibility you have over your mood and hands the keys to your emotions to an external force that evidently can't be trusted to hold them.

After hearing Adam rattle off that miserable moan about his invoice one more time, I finally looked up from my laptop and asked him to come over and talk with me.

'What's going on, mate?' I asked. He explained how this New York client never paid on time and how it had now ruined his chances of being able to book a holiday, and how that meant that his girlfriend would be upset, especially considering that she'd had a rough time lately, and that would make it worse, and so their relationship would be on the rocks and how if their relationship broke down, it would be a pain in the arse to find somewhere to live and how that might mean he had to move home and how if he moved home . . .

'STOP!' I interjected. 'Show me your invoices.'

He pulled up the last three invoices he had sent to his New York client on his laptop. A quick scan of the invoices highlighted a few alarming things. He had not specified the invoice due date on any of them (he said he assumed this information was obvious) and they looked terribly amateur – no company branding, poor formatting and ambiguous terminology. I sat with him for five minutes as we re-did his invoice template, adding a clear and obvious payment date, re-formatting it to look more professional and adding a late payment charge for good measure. 'Use this from now on,' I said, as I returned my focus to my laptop.

Fast forward three months and I receive an email from Adam. 'Hey bro, thank you again for helping me with my invoice situation. Since you tweaked it, they've never missed a payment date. Ha! Legend.'

If, when you get angry, you say 'X thing made me angry' you will get angry often.

If you say 'I made myself angry because of X thing' you will get angry less often.

Your emotional response is your fault and responsibility. If you realise that, you'll have the power to control it.

What is the moral of this story? One word – responsibility. The older I've become, and the further I've travelled in the business world, the more glaringly obvious it's become to me that a key difference between the 'happiest, sexiest millionaires' – the most fulfilled, romantically prosperous and successful people – and the most unhappy, romantically ineffective, broke people, is the former's ability and willingness to take responsibility. Humans are experts at taking responsibility for the great things that happen to them. You became a millionaire? 'Yes, I'm self-made!' You wrote a great book? 'Yes, all my ideas!' You won a bet? 'Yes, I knew that would happen!' But when life delivers misfortune, failure and hardship, taking responsibility becomes an impossible task for many. Who wants to take responsibility for not making rent, for getting fired, for gaining weight, for failing their driving test, for being dumped? No one.

If Adam says to himself 'X thing made me angry', then he will get angry more often and he'll stay angry for longer periods of time. If he learns to reframe that sentence as 'I made myself angry because of X thing' he will get angry less often and stay angry for shorter periods of time.

Our emotional response is our fault and responsibility. If we're able to realise that, we have the power to control it. If we don't, like a hijacked plane, someone or something else will. Having control over your emotional responses means you can think, respond and act with reason and clarity, and rational thinking is far more conducive to successful outcomes.

Admitting to fault, failure, weakness, inexperience or naivety turns an uncomfortable mirror on ourselves in a way that a fragile ego or delicate self-esteem can't always bear. If Nir Eyal is right, and we do live our lives avoiding psychological discomfort, then maybe our knee-jerk refusal to accept responsibility is a defence mechanism against a potential assault on our self-image.

Paradoxically, in trying to 'defend' ourselves, the science says we're attacking our chances of happiness, success and progress.

If you believe that you have control and responsibility over what happens in your life then you have what psychologists refer to as an 'internal locus of control'. If you believe that you have no control over what happens and that external variables are to blame, then you have what is known as an 'external locus of control'. Your locus of control can influence not only how you respond to the events that happen in your life, but also your motivation to take action when it matters the most. If you believe that you hold the keys to your fate, you are more likely to do what is necessary to change your situation when needed. If, on the other hand, you believe that the outcome is out of your hands, you may be less likely to work towards change and less likely to assess situations objectively in order to improve, like Adam.

The science tells an important story about those who have an internal or external locus of control.

Internal locus of control	**External locus of control**
•Are more likely to take responsibility for their actions.	•Blame outside forces for their circumstances.
•Tend to be less influenced by the opinions of other people.	•Often credit luck or chance for any successes.
•Often do better at tasks when they are allowed to work at their own pace.	•Don't believe that they can change their situation through their own efforts.
•Usually, have a strong sense of self-efficacy.	•Frequently feel hopeless or powerless in the face of difficult situations.
•Tend to work hard to achieve the things they want.	•Are more prone to experiencing learned helplessness.
•Feel confident in the face of challenges.	
•Tend to be physically healthier.	
•Report being happier and more independent.	
•Often achieve greater success in the workplace.	

Note that locus of control is a continuum. No one has a 100 per cent external or internal locus of control. Instead, most people lie somewhere between the two extremes.

Research has suggested that men tend to have a higher internal locus of control than women – likely a consequence of social conditioning – and that locus of control tends to become more internal as people grow older.

It's clear that Adam had a very external locus of control on that day. As he moaned about what had happened to him and attributed blame to an external party, he voluntarily became a helpless victim. The answer to his predicament was just one Google search or word of advice away the whole time, but because he had relinquished control and had sought refuge in catastrophising, the solution eluded him.

I had 700 team members working for me at Social Chain, and with that enlightening perspective I could see an undeniable pattern in the 'locus of control' of those who progressed the fastest and those who were professionally stagnant. Those with a strong internal locus of control were commercially more successful, better able to deal with adversity and ultimately made for great managers and directors. Those who only took responsibility for their victories, and engaged in blame, scape-goating and excuses for problems and failures were the least commercially successful and emotionally resilient. They were usually unable to progress to managerial roles.

I know that a key reason I was in the position where I had 700 employees is because of my own uncompromising internal locus of control and sense of personal responsibility. When I was an 18-year-old university drop-out living in a boarded-up house in an area known for gun crime, when my parents weren't speaking to me and I had no money, no job and no degree –

99% of the harm is caused in your head, by you and your thoughts.

1% of the harm is caused by reality, what actually happens and the outcome.

Most of the time, the problem isn't the problem. The way you think about the problem is.

---

what I did have was a sense of personal responsibility. I knew I was in that position because of me and because of my choices. The government didn't put me there, bad luck didn't put me there and my parents didn't put me there. I put myself there. And because I knew that I put myself there, I also knew I had the power and control to put myself somewhere else, somewhere like where I am right now. In my most desperate impoverished moments, I blamed nobody and I know, for sure, that if I had blamed external forces for my situation, I would likely still be there. Because if I didn't view my circumstances as controllable, then why on earth would I have tried to control them? That's insanity.

A certain type of person fucking hates it when I say this – it makes them uncomfortable because it turns the mirror of responsibility in their direction. Unfortunately, personal responsibility for your circumstances has become selectively controversial and seemingly political. I say selectively controversial because we all agree that some people's actions are directly responsible for their circumstances (e.g. criminals in jail), but we dare not apply the same standard of personal responsibility to the clinically obese, someone who's been fired from their job or someone who's bankrupt.

Of course, there's important nuance in all of these examples, but that doesn't mean that the party in question shouldn't take responsibility for the situation they find themselves in. Those who take personal responsibility have a greater chance of positive change; those who alleviate personal responsibility have less scope for doing so.

I DIDN'T EXPECT TO TALK ABOUT POLITICS, BUT HERE WE ARE . . .

I've always tended to avoid talking about politics, especially during my time as a CEO. It felt like a lose–lose topic considering my position and the political diversity of our company. Our left-leaning employees were always the most publicly vocal, our right-leaning employees were equally passionate, but less overtly vocal. However, this is a book, not a virtue-signalling social network where people are waiting in the wings with their 'whataboutry' to rebut a 280-character point of view, so maybe, just maybe, I can share some of my general uncategorisable views here.

I grew up liberal with left-leaning views. If you look at the vast majority of my political views, you might say that I 'belong' to the 'left'. However, the one factor above all others that's driven me towards the centre over the last five years is the left's tendency to grab hold of narrow-minded, responsibility-avoiding narratives. The implied narrative that all rich people are undeserving, evil, selfish and lucky. The implied narrative that hard work doesn't matter at all and that your circumstances are entirely the consequence of the government, or good or bad fortune, and the narrative that if a conservative/right-leaning political party is in power then 'we're all fucked', as one of my leftist friends tweeted.

I'm repulsed by these narratives because they're so binary and intent on avoiding personal responsibility by establishing an external locus of control. As much as I believe in our society offering everyone a safety net, higher taxes on the wealthy and universal healthcare, I can't sign up to narratives that seek to externalise my sense of accountability, vilify success or encourage victimhood. I just can't. If I did, if I became that type of person – someone who indulges in irrational blame and evades personal responsibility – the science would suggest that I would not be as happy, love would be harder to find and professional success would be more difficult than it already is.

So what am I? What political party do I belong to? Which box do I fit in? Once again, I probably don't, and once again, I'm totally fine with that. I'm just a guy, not a label. And I think that's a good thing, because the more we see the world's complex problems in a binary way (Police vs The People, Black vs White, Left vs Right, Men vs Women, Poor vs Rich), the less effective a binary perspective will be at fixing them.

Chapter Seventeen

I AM JUST AS UNMOTIVATED AS YOU ARE, HERE'S THE DIFFERENCE

IF YOU READ one of those articles online about 'the habits of highly successful people' and then look at how I've lived my life over the last five years, it would seem quite remarkable that I've attained the level of success I have, at the age that I have.

I'm not one of those superhuman robots that I often read about, one of those mythical super-entrepreneurs who springs up out of bed at 4am, drinks green juice, meditates, journals and goes for a one-hour run every morning without fail. I tend to believe those articles and the narratives of perfection that they promote are naive, dishonest and unhelpful.

Let me be honest for a second. I'm disorganised. I don't like getting out of bed and I don't routinely meditate. If I don't have an urgent meeting that I have to wake up for I won't set an alarm – I'll wake up whenever I wake up. Sometimes I eat healthily and sometimes I eat shit; sometimes I'm disciplined and sometimes I struggle. My sleeping patterns are all over the place, usually determined by my schedule, not vice versa. I procrastinate, get distracted easily and spend too much time down internet rabbit holes. If they had the guts to be honest with you, this is probably the case for 99 per cent of 'successful' people. If this admission has made you think less of me, that means your perception of me was just inaccurate to begin with.

Based on the assumption that my success is a consequence of unwavering motivation, I'm often asked, 'How do you stay motivated all the time?' The answer I give is, as you've probably guessed, 'I don't.' Nobody is motivated all of the time and I'm certainly not 'motivated' to do a lot of the things that I have to do.

Motivation is a poorly described concept that has been largely defined by those with an incentive to depict it in a certain way, to simplify it for clicks or to distort it for respect. Here is pretty much everything I know about the true nature of motivation . . .

YOUR GOALS, YOUR HAPPINESS, YOUR REGRETS

Intrinsic motivations come from within, while extrinsic motivations arise from outside of us. When you're intrinsically motivated, you engage in an activity solely because you enjoy it and get personal satisfaction from it. When you're extrinsically motivated, you do something in order to gain an external reward, such as money, recognition or in the avoidance of trouble, such as losing a job.

Social media, our parents, traditional media, adverts, pop culture and other forms of extrinsic social conditioning have influenced all of us to believe there is a 'correct' thing for us to become. Your mum and dad might have told you that's a lawyer or a doctor. Social media might say it's an influencer, entrepreneur,

YouTuber or philanthropist. Traditional media might suggest an athlete or an actor. Adverts may have told you it's a model while pop culture might want you to be a rapper.

In addition to this external 'correct' answer, there's also an internal 'correct' answer – a thing(s) inside you that you truly want to become, an interest(s) you're uniquely skilled to pursue, a person you would intrinsically love to be, 'work' you would never consider as work, a light from your younger years that adulthood has been unable to extinguish, a career(s) you would love to chase or a life that you would instinctively love to live. Maybe you want to paint in the mountains of Costa Rica, write your own cookery book, become a pilot, build cars in Silicon Valley, work with animals in India, record an album, dance or teach history?

The influence that external social conditioning has over us has evolved and intensified over the past two decades. The advent of the internet, social media and the algorithms they're driven by have changed the way we see the world, how often we see the world and how accurately we see the world. Social media metrics (the likes, comments and followers) have become barometers that determine how well we're playing the role that the outside world tells us to play. More people say that they want to be entrepreneurs, influencers, gamers, millionaires, public speakers, self-help gurus and fashion models now than ever before. This is because the internet tells us that those pursuits are the 'correct' ones, the most admirable and validating pursuits and, therefore, apparently the most fulfilling.

Most of us now find ourselves at war with our external and internal 'correct' answers and too often, we struggle to know which is which. If the external pressure to be a 'happy sexy millionaire' is strong and your need for external validation is high, then your intrinsic desires stand no chance of being heard, pursued or achieved, and you will live your life genuinely believing that you want something you don't actually want – something that won't actually truly fulfil you. It's only upon achieving that extrinsic goal that you'll realise, as I did, how empty it ultimately is.

Similarly, if the pressure from your parents to be a doctor is non-negotiable and your wish to please them is intense, then your intrinsic desire to be a ballet dancer stands no chance and you risk living your life genuinely believing that you want to be a doctor, mindlessly pursuing that goal until a mid-life crisis informs you of what you already knew deep down – you should have been a dancer.

You must interrogate the logic, values and rationale behind your goals and ambitions as if your life depended on it – because it does. The truth is that most people don't know the difference between their intrinsic goals and their extrinsic goals. When asked what their goals are, I frequently hear enthusiastic young people tell me that they want to 'change the world'. Although admirable on the surface, that clearly isn't an intrinsic goal; it is one potential outcome of an accomplished intrinsic goal.

They don't actually want to 'change the world', they want the admiration, status and self-esteem boost that they believe are on offer. If they actually wanted to change the world, they would be focused on a goal, not a reward. They would say 'I want to work in the electric vehicle industry' or 'I want to do clinical research on cancer treatments' or 'I want to work in aerospace technology'. That genuine and specific aspiration is nearly always the starting point for the eventual worldwide admiration that world-changing entrepreneurs, inventors and philanthropists achieve.

Things you will regret:

1) Allowing your potential to remain trapped behind strangers' opinions.
2) Spending more time thinking about the past than living in the moment.
3) Time spent with people that don't want the best for you.
4) Neglecting family.
5) Never taking risks.

—

As I said earlier, this generation are too quick to conflate their external admiration (for the 'successful' people they follow on Instagram) with their internal aspirations for themselves, their lives and their future. This is a mistake that will cost both the motivation they need to become successful people themselves and the happiness on offer in pursuing their own personal goals.

When our intrinsic desires lose, so do we.

The science couldn't be clearer on this. A 2009 study asked 147 recent college grads to report their aspirations in life and their happiness or unhappiness. Their intrinsic aspirations included close relationships, community involvement, personal growth and professional ambitions. Their extrinsic aspirations included money, fame and having an appealing public image.

The results were undeniable. The students who realised their intrinsic goals had high levels of happiness whereas those who attained their extrinsic goals saw no improvement in their happiness. The researchers theorise that people who pursue extrinsic goals may feel momentarily satisfied after reaching their goals, but it almost never lasts.

With that said, it's clearly so unbelievably important to know what you actually want, who you actually are, and to be able to tell the difference between the person the outside world wants you to be, and the person your inside world yearns for you to become.

You may have heard of Bronnie Ware, an Australian nurse who cared for people who had been sent home to die. She was with them for the last three to twelve weeks of their lives at a time when they were reflective, remorseful and sometimes fearful. When questioned about any regrets they had or anything they would do differently, common themes surfaced again and again. In Bronnie's book, *The Top Five Regrets of the Dying*, she reveals that the most common and consistent regret her patients expressed was 'I wish I'd had the courage to live a life true to myself, not the life others expected of me'. Of all the things a dying person could regret about their life, that was it: living an extrinsically motivated life, and not the life they wanted deep within.

When I read this it hit me like a tonne of bricks. There's a powerful retrospective clarity one must have as they approach their final days. I'm not there yet, hopefully you're not there yet, but if this was the most common regret expressed by Bronnie's dying patients, then listen. Regret is such an awful thing, a haunting and often irreversible mistake. Please avoid it. Please live your life on your terms, unapologetically chasing *you.* It's your life and it's going to be your regret, so it has to be your decision.

BURNT OUT AND UNMOTIVATED

If you try to become someone else or live someone else's life – one that isn't true to you – you'll also struggle to find the motivation you'll need to succeed at it, and sooner or later you'll likely encounter an unpleasant thing that our society calls 'burnout'.

There's been a lot said about what burnout actually is, and what causes it. To me, one of the main causes is the relentless pursuit of those external goals, i.e. if you're working long hours for years at a job that you don't truly enjoy just because it pays well, then you're on the road to burnout. I say this because I've never experienced burnout when doing things I honestly enjoyed doing, regardless of how many hours I give to it. People don't seem to get burnt out from watching their favourite football team play, creating art for pleasure or playing games they enjoy. But if you spend long enough pursuing those extrinsic goals, for extrinsic rewards, burnout seems somewhat inevitable.

"SOME PEOPLE DIE AT 25 AND AREN'T BURIED UNTIL 75."

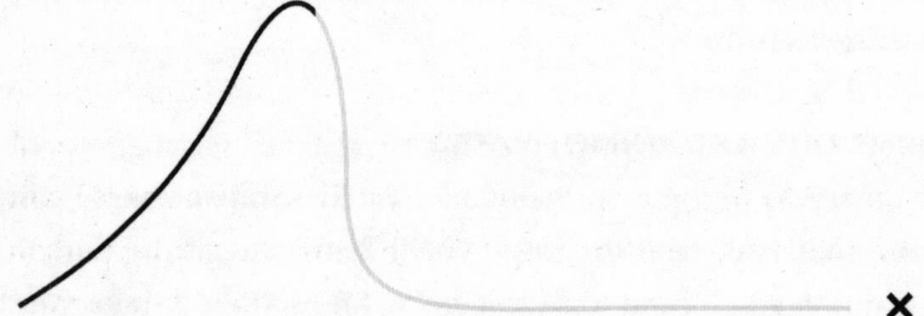

BENJAMIN FRANKLIN

Between the ages of 11 and 18 I, like most of you, was placed in the higher-education system – the most boring place on earth. That meant that I – a curious, practical and energetic kid – spent seven hours a day for eight years locked inside a small white box listening to some overworked and underpaid teacher trying to engage me until a sympathetic bell granted my freedom. People wonder why my attendance hit 30 per cent and I was ultimately expelled from school! It was painfully boring. I had no intrinsic motivation to attend, or to do my homework – ever.

That same kid would then spend the following seven years, between the ages of 18 and 25, working relentlessly, showing up every day, doing his homework and building one of the marketing industry's most impressive companies of the last decade. Perhaps it might seem I was lazy and then I grew out of it, but that's not the case. I was never inherently lazy. I, like you, am just not interested in doing things, for long periods of time, that I'm not intrinsically motivated to do. When I am aligned with my inner dreams, I'm the hardest-working person on planet Earth. Then I'm able to achieve the all-important consistency I preached about in Chapter 14 and, like a river cutting through a canyon, the results are awe-inspiring – unlike my grades in school, D, C, D, E, B . . . I can't even remember.

YOU'RE THE ONLY GREAT PERSON YOU CAN BECOME

The truth is: none of us actually want to be a sexy, famous millionaire. We don't want a pile of stuff, we don't want a sports car and we do not want a mansion. We just fundamentally want the thing that we believe those items are going to do for us – we want to feel how we think those things are going to make us feel. At the most fundamental level we all just want to be happy. We mistakenly think stuff, status and external approval will get us there. But it's the intrinsic things like

If you try to be someone else, you'll become nobody at all. The only great person you have the possibility of becoming is the greatest version of yourself, and that is a pretty great person.

---

friendships, internal fulfilment and our honest passions that ultimately hold the key to happiness.

They also seem to hold the key to success. If you strive for intrinsically driven goals, you'll have the motivation to help you to achieve consistency, avoid burnout and edge closer to mastery. It turns out that the only way to become great yourself is by living your life your way, for your reasons.

Life has come to teach me that if you try to be someone else, you'll just increase your chances of becoming nobody at all. After all, the only great person you have the possibility of becoming is the greatest version of yourself, and that is a pretty great person.

IF THEY PAY YOU TO DO IT, IT MIGHT BE HARDER TO DO

It's so important to be aware of the influence that external rewards have on your internal goals. The minute you allow money to become the driving motivator behind a once intrinsically motivating goal, your motivation is actually at risk and the chance of you achieving that goal will diminish. I'll say that again in simple terms: if someone pays you to do something you love doing, you'll lose some of the motivation to do it.

In the 1970s psychologists explored the relationship between our self-driven (or intrinsic) motivation and outside influences (extrinsic motivation).Their research highlighted what psychologists would call the 'undermining effect': if you provide incentives for someone to carry out an activity they already enjoy, it undermines their original reason for doing it.

In an experiment two randomly split groups of participants were asked to perform an interesting task – one they naturally enjoyed – but only one of the groups was told that they would be paid as a reward if they performed well. Later on, participants were asked to choose a task without any reward. Participants from the earlier reward group were less likely to pick up the same task if they cease to be rewarded for it. Participants who were not rewarded to do that task before, were more likely to pick it again. In other words, the payment seemed to undermine their intrinsic motivation to do that activity. This psychological phenomenon has subsequently been witnessed across many experiments by multiple researchers.

You may be able to relate to this – I know I certainly can. I tend to lose motivation to do something when that thing becomes more about rewards than internal fulfilment. Public speaking, my personal brand, producing content – whenever these things have become driven by money and not the internal enjoyment I get from doing them, they've surprisingly become harder to do. The larger my social media channels became, and the more it became about likes, followers, money and external rewards, the less motivation I found to run them.

The 'undermining effect' finds its explanation in something called the 'self-determination theory'. Self-determination describes people's desire to feel in control of their own lives. It might seem like intrinsic motivation and extrinsic motivation are diametrically opposed – with intrinsic motivations driving behaviour in keeping with our 'real self' and extrinsic leading us to conform with the standards of others – but there is another important distinction in these types of motivation that the self-determination theory explores.

We are complex beings who are rarely driven by only one type of motivation. Different goals, desires and ideas inform us of what we want and need, therefore it is useful to think of motivation not as a binary concept, but a concept that lives on a continuum ranging from 'non-self-determined' (things you're forced to do) to 'self-determined' (things you choose to do).

Never trade your happiness for a career, money, external validation, popularity or status.

The ultimate goal is happiness.

Your wealth, success, fame and accomplishments will only be worthwhile if they served that goal.

Although self-determination is generally the goal for individuals, we can't help but be motivated by external sources – and that's not always a bad thing. Both intrinsic and extrinsic motivation are highly influential determinants of our behaviour, and both drive us to meet the 'three basic needs' identified by the self-determination theory model:

The Self-Determination continuum

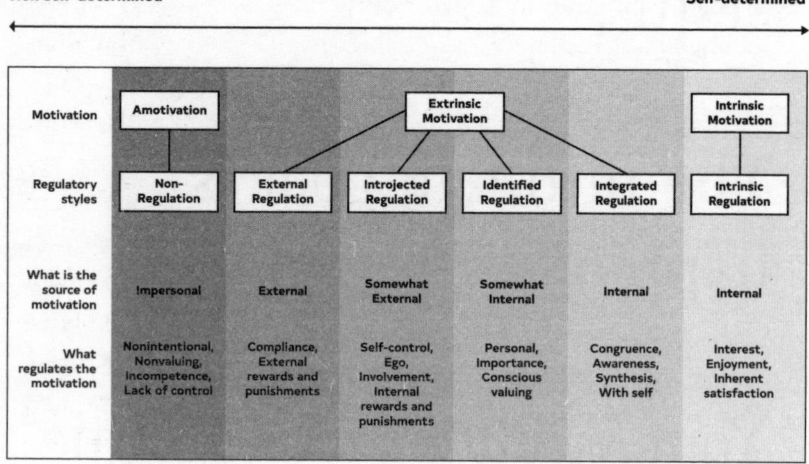

1. Autonomy: people have a need to feel that they are the masters of their own destiny and that they have at least some control over their lives; most importantly, people have a need to feel that they are in control of their own behaviour.
2. Competence: another need concerns our achievements, knowledge and skills; people have a need to build their competence and develop mastery over tasks that are important to them.
3. Connection: people need to have a sense of belonging and connectedness with others; each of us needs other people to some degree.

HOW I BECAME AN UNMOTIVATED INSTAGRAM BOYFRIEND

My ex-girlfriend was a bit of an Instagram model and that meant that when we went on holiday, I became one of those Instagram photographer boyfriends, scaling rocks, crouching down and achieving the stillness of a sniper in order to get that perfect shot. I loved taking photos of her – I knew it helped her and I loved taking pictures anyway, so whenever she asked me, I was more than happy to help. A few months into our relationship while in Jamaica on holiday, she passed me the phone and asked me to take a few snaps of her in a bikini as part of a brand deal she had to fulfil.

I crouched down, did my usual 100+ snaps and passed back the phone. As she swiped through my work, I could see her becoming increasingly despondent. Her casual disappointment became a frown, and then the frown become an audible tut of disapproval. A few days later, she asked me to take photos of her again. I obliged, took over 100 photos and passed the phone back. Once again, she swiped through the photos visibly disappointed and frustrated. She handed the phone back to me, and proceeded to irritably direct me, position me and tell me precisely how each photo should be taken.

Two days later, the same routine commenced. She passed me her phone and asked me to take photos of her. This time, however, my instinctive reaction was different. I didn't want to; I dreaded the task and I asked her if she could set the camera up on a timer and take the pictures herself. It wasn't that I didn't want to help her – I did – I loved helping her. It's just that I felt like I couldn't please her, that I was doing something wrong. I now felt bad taking photos of her. A task I used to enjoy doing and was always motivated to do had become a feared chore, just because the feedback I had received from her was continually negative.

And herein lies another important factor in terms of motivation – interpersonal exchanges, rewards, communication and feedback that gear you towards feelings of competence when performing an activity have been proven to enhance your intrinsic motivation for that particular activity. Continual negative feedback, which makes you question your competence when performing a task, is one of the biggest killers of motivation.

The boost in motivation that can be achieved from positive feedback and feelings of competence, though, is only achieved if the individual feels that the performance of the task was their autonomous, independent, free choice.

So, for a high level of intrinsic motivation two psychological needs have to be fulfilled:

1. Competence – so that the activity results in feelings of self-development and success.
2. Autonomy and freedom.

My ex-girlfriend made me feel both incompetent through her feedback and unable to utilise any degree of autonomy through her precise micro-management. If you've ever had a partner like this or an arsehole manager who criticised often and micro-managed you incessantly, I know you'll be able to relate. If you want to motivate someone, be positive and constructive with your feedback. You don't need to blow smoke up their arse if they don't deserve the praise, but if your criticisms are geared towards constructive self-development, and not personal or ambiguous critique, then you'll be fine.

This also explains why researchers continually find that money or extrinsic rewards undermine intrinsic motivation, and why I became less motivated to post on my social media channels when I finally had millions of followers and a commercial incentive to do so. These external rewards undermine your autonomy – and your behaviour starts to become controlled by the rewards, not by you.

We explored the importance of taking responsibility in the last chapter, but this point about autonomy inspiring motivation brings it back into focus. It explains why those who have high feelings of personal responsibility – and believe that their actions determine their outcomes – are typically the most motivated, because if you don't feel like you have control over the outcome then, according to psychology, you're less likely to have the motivation to do the task in question. I mean, what's the point? If you don't feel like you have control anyway, why bother?

With all we've explored in this chapter, let me try to conclude. The most motivated version of you or me, someone that is considered high in 'self-determination', is reaching for a goal that we internally genuinely care about, a goal that is consistent with our authentic values and a goal we're able to pursue with freedom, autonomy and personal responsibility. If you get constructive positive feedback and feel competent in your pursuit of that goal, even better.

For example, imagine a high-school student fails an important test. If she is high in self-determination and therefore motivation, she will feel responsible for her actions and believe she is in control of her behaviour; she might tell her parents that she could have spent more time studying and that she plans to create some extra time to study and to re-take the test. Her plan of action would be the same whether her parents were upset or apathetic, because she herself is motivated by an internal desire to get good grades, be competent and knowledgeable – that intrinsically and authentically matters to her.

Love does not seek to control or dominate.

Good leaders do not seek to control or dominate.

True friends do not seek to control or dominate. Insecurity does.

If this same student is low in self-determination, she would feel that she is not in control of her life and a victim of circumstance. She could blame the school for giving her a tough test that she wasn't ready for. She may blame her tutor for not helping her study or her friends for distracting her. If she cares about her grade, it is not due to an internal desire to do well (intrinsic reasons), but perhaps a desire to win her parents' approval or perhaps boost her self-image by getting the best grade in the class or impressing her teacher with her knowledge (extrinsic reasons). She probably won't opt to re-sit the test, as she won't feel that her own actions were responsible for the outcome.

Similarly, the man who decides to start a new hobby because he thinks he'll enjoy it is exhibiting self-determination, while the man who begins a new hobby because it seems prestigious or impressive is not. A woman who blames all of her ex-lovers for ruining their relationships is not displaying self-determination; the woman who takes responsibility for her part in contributing to unhappy past relationships is showing self-determination.

You will have spotted the theme here: those who take responsibility for their actions and do things because they align with their own personal values and goals are self-determined and motivated. Those who blame others, see themselves as constant victims and do things solely for external approval or recognition, are not.

Knowing what you truly care about, and knowing who you truly are, is becoming more and more difficult, given the increasing number of authoritative external forces that are gradually and deliberately sculpting you into something and somebody you aren't. It's your job to fight back, to hear your internal voice through the noise and to make that voice the most influential one in your life. If you can, you'll find happiness. Add a serving of responsibility, freedom and some feelings of competence and you'll find motivation.

Chapter Eighteen

HOW TO BECOME THE BEST IN THE WORLD AT SOMETHING WHILE BEING THE BEST IN THE WORLD AT . . . NOTHING

ONE OF MY friends is widely considered to be one of the best photographers in the world – he's certainly paid as such. If you're into photography, there is a high chance you'll know of him and his work. He has an enormous, mind-blowing, four-storey studio in the heart of London, and he's personally photographed anyone who is anyone: the Queen, Barack Obama, Madonna, Kate Moss, you name them.

However, when you look at his technical photography knowledge, his business acumen, his branding aptitude, his marketing abilities or his social media proficiency, he's not the best in the world at any of those individual skills. He's probably in the top 10 per cent in his industry at all of those things – an 8 out of 10 across all of them.

Access to information is the real privilege.

Money is a fish. Information is a fishing rod.

Only one of them will feed you for a lifetime.

In the world we live in, we all have access to information, but most of us still don't understand the true value of it.

In fact, I have another friend called Dan who I think is actually a better technical photographer than him, although Dan doesn't excel at everything else.

Until I met my best-photographer-in-the-world friend, I used to think that you had to be the best in the world at an individual skill in order to be the best in the world in your industry. I used to think that if you wanted to become the best entrepreneur in the world, you needed to know the most about the topic of business, or if you wanted to be the best chef in the world you needed to cook the best food in the world. It turns out I was wrong, and the realisation that I was wrong, and why I was wrong, changed my life forever and completely shifted my self-development and career focus.

THE ART OF SKILL STACKING

There are few pursuits in life that require mastery of just one key skill; chess might be one example. To be the world's best chess player, you just need to be the best at chess. That's virtually impossible to do considering the fact that over 600 million people play the game and genetic factors are considered to have an important positive influence on the very top players. However, the rest of our lives, careers and professional ambitions are multifaceted, and success doesn't depend on mastering one skill.

Two years ago, in an annual vote which polled 100 leaders from my industry, I was voted as the #1 leading figure in social media marketing. It was a huge compliment, but one that I struggled to understand. I don't consider myself to be the best at any individual part of the social media marketing game – I had built a big company but there are bigger companies, I am really good at the technical aspect of social media marketing but I knew people who were a little better. I was good at the business side but, again, I knew people who were better at business. It wasn't until I read about the concept of 'skill stacking', which was initially popularised by author Scott Adams, the creator of the Dilbert cartoons, that I began to understand the reason why my industry considered me the best.

In chess, you become the best by being the best at one skill. However, our careers are much more complex and they're almost never defined by mastery of any one skill – they're defined by our ability to be pretty good at a bunch of uniquely complementary skills.

I was really good at the technical aspects of social media marketing, running a business, personal branding, being visionary, writing, public speaking and sales. I wasn't the best in the world at any of those skills on their own, but I was most certainly in the top 5–10 per cent of each of them. This is how skill stacking works. It's actually easier and more effective to be in the top 10 per cent in several different skills – your 'stack' – than it is to be in the top 1 per cent in any one skill.

Let's run some numbers on this. If your city has a million people, for example, and you belong in the top 10 per cent of six different skills, that's 1,000,000 x 10% x 10% x 10% x 10% x 10% x 10% = 1. That makes you the number-one person in your city with those six skills. Bump that number up to 10 skills? Boom, you're the best in the city at that combination of 10 skills.

This means that, statistically, to become the best in your industry you do not need to become the best at any one aspect, you just need to be very good at a variety of complementary skills – skills that your industry requires for personal success. The more unique the skills, the better.

In my industry, very few social media CEOs understood the

power and art of personal branding as well as me; those who did weren't typically also great at business. Those who were the best at business weren't typically great public speakers, and those who were great at public speaking usually didn't understand the technical aspects of social media marketing. The CEOs that understood the technical aspects of social media marketing often made for better employees than visionary CEOs. What I'm trying to say is, in order to be considered the best in my industry, I didn't have to become the best at anything, I just had to be good at six to seven of the right, complementary and uniquely rare things. This is a theme that runs true with nearly all industry leaders.

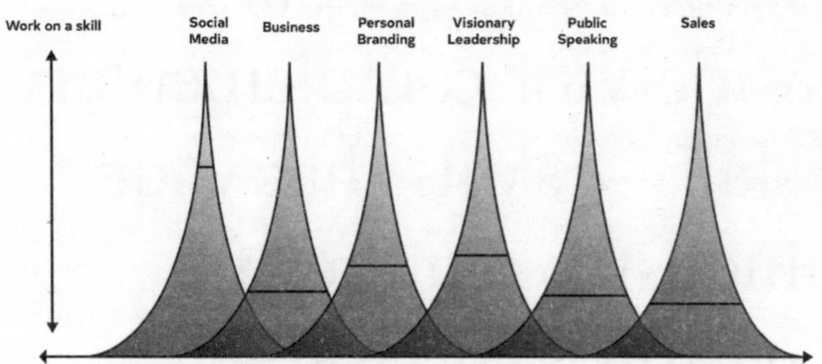

As you can see, in my skill stack I'm in the top 5 per cent at several things, but I'm in the top 1 per cent in the technical aspect of social media marketing. Although it's valuable to have specific knowledge, to me my specific knowledge is the least valuable skill I have in the long term because it's the most teachable, the least transferable and specific knowledge decays in relevance faster than fundamental skills.

This means that, statistically, to become the best in your industry you do not need to become the best at any one aspect, you just need to be very good at a variety of complementary skills – skills that your industry requires for personal success.

The skills I value the most are key transferable skills like sales, public speaking and personal branding. Being capable in those core skills means I'll have a fundamental advantage in many industries, and also when the world inevitably changes and all that I know about social media marketing becomes redundant.

This is summarised succinctly in the book *The Almanack of Naval Ravikant*:

> Knowing how to be persuasive when speaking is far more important than being an expert digital marketer or click optimizer. Foundations are key. It's much better to be at 9/10 or 10/10 on foundations than to try to get super deep into things, but you do need to be deep in something because otherwise you'll be a mile wide and an inch deep and you won't get what you want out of life.

When building your own skill stack, complementary and unique skills are incredibly important. Steve Jobs and the company he created in Apple is a great example of this. At the heart of Jobs' skill stack is a passion for design, be it fonts, packaging or architecture. Talking about how attending a calligraphy class at Reed College contributed to his success with Apple, he said:

> I decided to take a calligraphy class to learn how to [do calligraphy]. I learned about serif and sans-serif type-faces, about varying the space between different letter

combinations, about what makes great typography great. It was beautiful. Historical. Artistically subtle in a way that science can't capture. And I found it fascinating. None of this had any hope of any practical application in my life. But ten years later, when we were designing the first Macintosh computer, it all came back to me. And we designed it all into the Mac. It was the first computer with beautiful typography. If I had never dropped in on that single course in college, the Mac would never have multiple typefaces or proportionally spaced fonts. And since Windows just copied the Mac, it's likely that no personal computer would have them.

"

This one rare skill, and the wider design knowledge which none of his competitors had, would ultimately set Apple and Steve apart in a way that would revolutionise his industry and the world. He was never the best in the world at design or calligraphy, but he had developed a keen understanding of winning design principles, and by combining his design skills with his unique deep insight into what people want, his tech knowledge, his rare strategic mind, his salesmanship, his computer science skills, his leadership skills and his business skills, he was able to build a company that was focused on advanced technology and beautiful design. That company felt different, better and more valuable because Steve's skill stack was different, better and ultimately more valuable. Jobs wasn't the best in the world at any of the skills within his skill stack, but the complementary and unique nature of his stack made his company the biggest and best in the world, and made him undeniably the best in his industry.

HOW YOU CAN BUILD AN INDUSTRY-DOMINATING SKILL STACK

When you consider the stack of skills you need to rise to the top of your industry, make sure you focus on unique and complementary skills. For example, if you're in the top 5 per cent at graphic design, being in the top 5 per cent at motion design isn't going to be a valuable differentiator. Most top graphic designers are good at both. You need to build skills that not only work together, but are also diverse enough to make you uniquely valuable.

Choose to build uniquely complementary skills that you don't often see in the same person. For example, computer coders aren't known to be great public speakers, visionary CEOs or talented salespeople. They're stereotypically more introverted and quieter, so those who can build great tech products, sell them and lead people already have a significant and valuable advantage.

This is often where people go wrong as they develop their skill stack over their careers. They avoid the calligraphy class because it 'doesn't make sense', they don't learn to code because they don't think they'll need it to be an artist, they evade public-speaking opportunities because they don't think it'll help them become a psychologist. Instead, they look at the skills possessed by the people in their industry already, and they focus on honing those. Their university teaches these, and their work experience in industry further reinforces, ultimately resulting in a completely predictable, common and lower-value skill stack.

As I said, becoming the best in the world at chess is virtually impossible and so it's hard to find the motivation to attempt such a feat. However, if you understand and believe in the concept of skill stacking, you really can change your life and career in a relatively short amount of time. You can go from knowing absolutely nothing about something to being quite skilled within a few months just by putting in a few hours of focused, deliberate daily practice. That's really all you need to start learning how to speak in public, get better at negotiation, pick up a new language, manage people better in a business environment, learn some useful new technology, code, draw, design, dance, play an instrument or start your own side hustle.

It's wise to go in search of new skills that you can stack to prepare yourself for the future – a future that promises to have technology and the internet at the heart of it. Those skills will increase your earnings and add variety to a career that may otherwise stagnate.

For me, the skills that set me apart the most as an entrepreneur are my social media skills, my public speaking skills and my sales skills. These were skills that the other social media marketing CEOs didn't have. I can't think of any other entrepreneurs in my industry and country who were able to, or knew how to, build a social media audience for themselves as I did. With over two million followers, and an ability to speak and sell eloquently, I was able to make my voice heard above all others. When you have the loudest and most persuasive voice and a high level of technical knowledge in an industry largely driven by the power of your authority, sales, social proofing and opinion, then you'll quickly rise to the top. My industry valued that skill stack, and so people like me and Gary Vaynerchuk – a friend of mine who shares a similar skill stack – both rose to the top of the social media marketing industry in our respective countries.

In order to build a unique, complementary and valuable skill stack you really need to know the answer to these questions:

1. What skills do you currently have?
2. In your industry, what skills do people usually have?
3. Given that most people have these skills, what new skills could you learn that will give you a valuable edge over others within your industry?

They say you can't teach an old dog new tricks, and innately we're all creatures of comfort and familiarity. But if you are willing to step outside of your zone of comfort into territories that someone like you doesn't usually explore, you too can build a skill stack capable of changing your life, eclipsing your industry and potentially even changing the world. You can become the best at something, without being the best at anything.

Chapter Nineteen

GAMBLING LIKE A HAPPY SEXY MILLIONAIRE

IF I'M FORTUNATE enough to live to 80 years old, I will have lived for about 29,200 days and 700,000 hours. Considering the fact that humans spend about 33 years of their lives in bed, that's really about 500,000 active hours. All I have is these 500,000 hours (if I'm lucky) – that is the gift that the Big Bang, God, or whatever you believe in, gave to both you and me. These 500,000 hours are fundamentally irreplaceable. If I spend some of them on my health and well-being, I may be able to earn a few more, but I'll never get back the ones I've spent. We can work harder or longer to earn more money. We can go to the supermarket to get more groceries. We can buy the latest and greatest gadgets. But, no matter how hard we try, we're stuck with an ever-diminishing amount of time.

We are all gamblers, stood over the roulette table of life. The one rule of the game is that we have to place one of our chips every hour and, once a chip is placed, we will never get it back. How we place these 500,000 chips will be the single biggest determining factor of our outcomes: our success, happiness, safety, legacy, intellectual development and mental well-being.

These 500,000 chips are all we fundamentally have, and everything that extrinsically seems to matter – our status, ego and material wealth – are just a consequence of these 500,000 chips. Once the game is over, we don't get to keep any of that stuff anyway.

I feel I need to really drill this point home, because I honestly don't believe that anyone truly understands this – including me. We don't seem to live as if time is all we have and that the time we have is limited. They say humans are incapable of understanding the concept of infinity, to grasp the idea of something that never ends – but maybe we're also incapable of understanding the concept of finality and the fact that we will at some point come to an end.

For a certain type of person, reading this chapter will be uncomfortable. We live in a culture that does its best to deny the reality of death – it remains a topic as taboo as sex was during the Victorian age. We seem to believe that death happens to other people, and we don't have the emotional fortitude to embrace the fact that it will happen to us. As Woody Allen put it, 'I'm not afraid of death. I just don't want to be there when it happens.'

When you observe how the vast majority of people live their lives, and how they allocate their 500,000 chips, it appears that they haven't consciously embraced the finite nature of time and the fact that at some point they will run out of chips.

You have a certain number of chips left right now. It could be one. Or if you're 30 years old, it's probably just over 300,000. If I placed a sand timer in front of you containing 300,000 hours of time, and that sand timer followed you wherever you went, it would undeniably change how you make your decisions, what you give your time to and how you fundamentally live your life.

‘We can work harder or longer to earn more money. We can go to the supermarket to get more groceries. We can buy the latest and greatest gadgets. But, no matter how hard we try, we’re stuck with an ever-diminishing amount of time.’
– Tom Stevenson

SAND TIMERS AND SACRIFICE

If you could see your precious, irreplaceable time pouring away through the neck of a sand timer, would you really spend hours mindlessly scrolling through social media timelines looking at strangers' selfies, engaging in petty gossip and drifting unconsciously down YouTube rabbit holes? Would you really spend time worrying about people pleasing, trivial issues, what others think about how you're living your life or fixated on winning worthless arguments with irrelevant people? Would you really choose to waste your chips and burden yourself with grudges, unforgiving people, bitterness and jealousy? I think and hope the answer is no.

Earlier, when I shared Bronnie Ware's recollections of the conversations she'd had with her dying patients, it illuminated the fact that people on their deathbeds were able to achieve a remarkable level of retrospective clarity and pinpoint what they should and shouldn't have done in their lives. They could accurately tell you what didn't matter and what should have mattered more, because they could now see their end in sight. That invisible finality was now visible, and it suddenly put everything, every decision and every hour, into context.

If you could see your sand timer, you would theoretically be able to see your end too – you would be able to visualise your time as finite and the true irreversible cost of every choice you make. In a world where time is unlimited – which is the world where I think most people mentally live – a bad decision, time wasted and dreams unfulfilled come at no significant fundamental cost. You can always correct that decision later, pursue that dream some other time or try again soon, we believe. In a world where your sand timer sits in front of you at all times, every choice you make or don't make is a visible sacrifice.

And here's the undeniable truth – backed by science, all of

human history and the inescapable laws of nature – your sand timer is there, right in front of you, right now, pouring away as you read these words. It's always been there and it always will be, but you will never see it. It will follow you wherever you go; it will never pause, stop or reverse.

I began to ponder this idea a few years ago, and it inspired me so much that I bought a sand timer for my desk at work, for my mantelpiece at home and for my bedside table. Once in a while I flip the sand timers, and I watch my time pouring away; it's one of the best ways I've found to visually see time – something that is otherwise impossible to do.

HOW WOULD WE LIVE OUR LIVES IF WE COULD SEE OUR SAND TIMERS?

Have you ever been to a death café? They've been popping up everywhere from Boston to Beijing, offering a congenial space where people gather to ponder mortality and the meaning of life over tea and cake. Having started in 2011, at the latest count nearly 3,000 death-café meetings have taken place in over 30 countries. The movement confronts an ancient existential dilemma: how should we live given that life is short, and time is running out on us?

Generations of scholars and sages have, of course, meditated on this question, from the Chinese philosopher Lao Tzu to the medieval theologian the Venerable Bede, from the Renaissance essayist Michel de Montaigne to the anthropologist Ernest Becker. One of the most recent figures on the scene – arguably a sage of the digital age – was the Venerable Steve Jobs.

In 2005 the Apple founder, who had just overcome a life-threatening battle with cancer, gave a commencement speech at Stanford University that went viral on YouTube under the title 'How to Live Before You Die'. Jobs, then 50 years old said; 'Remembering I'll be dead soon is the most important tool I've ever encountered to help me make the big choices in life.'

Having survived this near-death experience (a relapse of the cancer took his life in 2011), he concluded that 'death is very likely the single best invention of life'. It can propel us to follow our dreams and intuition, to defy convention, to take risks and to pursue our own path. 'Your time is limited,' Jobs told the assembled students, 'so don't waste it living someone else's life.'

Two millennia earlier, the Roman Emperor Marcus Aurelius pronounced that: 'Perfection of character is this: to live each day as if it were your last, without frenzy, without apathy, without pretence.'

Another Stoic thinker, the philosopher Seneca, lamented in his book *On The Shortness of Life* that 'it is not that we have a short space of time, but that we waste so much of it . . .' His advice? The wise man 'plans out every day as if it were his last'.

It's clear that the cliché of 'living every day as if it were your last' is terrible short-term advice. Of course, you shouldn't live every day as if you had just one day left. If you did, the chances are your decisions would be terribly destructive – I know I'd be morbidly obese, toothless and probably broke. However, this isn't what these great minds were inherently promoting, they were stressing the importance of understanding how scarce and limited your time is and treating it as such – they were trying to put your sand timer in front of you in order to help you prioritise and focus.

How would you live your life if you could see your sand timer pouring away?

BECOMING A MASTER OF NO

I guess that really is the ultimate conclusion and remedy to all of this. The importance of prioritisation and focus. But how do we know what to prioritise and focus on right now?

Answering this question starts with a subjective analysis of your own values. Start by becoming crystal clear about the things, ambitions and goals you deeply value above all else. What are the things you're willing to sacrifice everything for – the finish line that is worth the marathon, and the mountain top that is worth the climb? In order to ensure these values are intrinsic, interrogate them relentlessly and as if your life depended on it. Demand to know the source of them, the reason for them and get clear about why those things matter to you.

For you it might be the mastery of a skill, to fix flaws you see in society, to create freedom of choice in your life and the lives of your children, to be healthier in your body and mind, to travel the world and create wonderful experiences, to pursue your passion for theatre, to be the best parent you can be, to educate, to inspire or to become spiritually enlightened. You decide, and don't let anyone belittle or trivialise the things you value.

Your intrinsic values should exist – by definition – free from the influence of external judgement. If you derive your fulfilment from playing video games, doodling or doing very little at all, then that's no less valid or subjectively important than Elon Musk's goal to send us to Mars or Steve Jobs' pursuit of a more connected world. But, whatever you value, you must be clear on it. If you're unclear, then things you don't value will overstay their welcome, steal your time and gradually push you away from your chances of a fulfilled life and towards the prospect of an unfulfilled one. The decisions you make should be rigorously cross-examined against these values.

Another way to interrogate your decisions in real time is by asking yourself, 'How would the person I want to become spend their time?' Or, 'Which decision would the person I want to become make right now?'

Going back to my roulette analogy, your goal is to place as many of your chips as you can on furthering these values every day, and to avoid placing any of them on things that are outside of these values. Achieving perfection here is both unreasonable and impossible, we all 'waste time' on things we shouldn't and time wasted is often only recognisable in hindsight. The goal is to place your chips with intention, as best as you can, today and to repeat that every day. When the wheel spins, you'll only win fulfilment from the chips you placed on the correct values – you risk regret from chips wasted.

It's easy to say yes to things we think we want to do or feel we should do. But when your currency is limited – like your time – your spending habits need to be policed meticulously; you need to budget, prioritise and be frugal.

In a practical sense, the more difficult yet equally important challenge is learning to say 'no' – even when it's something that you want to do. Right now, I really want to watch the football that I know I'm missing while writing this book. I also want to walk over to McDonald's and get a Big Mac. But I'm choosing to say no to both of those things because this book is more important according to my intrinsic values, and I know that any attempt to do the above would ultimately be chips placed on things outside of my sincerest, most critical long-term values.

How would the person you want to become spend their time?

Once you have clarity on what your values are, you then have to continually reverse engineer those values back to your decisions today, in this moment, right now.

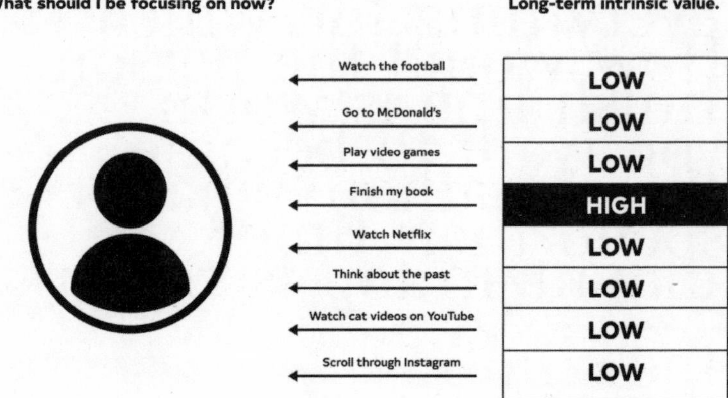

In every moment of our lives, we're surrounded by an almost endless number of decision pathways. Navigating to things that offer high levels of long-term intrinsic value and avoiding short-term temptations, distractions and our innate instinct to steer clear of discomfort isn't always easy.

The more successful I became, the more people and opportunities demanded my chips and the more ruthless I had to become in placing them. It turns out this strict focus makes you even more successful, which increases the demand on your chips and the cycle continues . . . It's gotten to the point now that if someone wants to book me to speak, make an appearance at their event or give them a professional consultation, my minimum fee is somewhere in the region of £10,000–£20,000 per hour.

What are the things you're willing to sacrifice everything for, which finish line is worth the marathon, what mountain top is worth the climb?

The most I've been paid as a fee for an hour's work is £90,000. You could theorise that it took me five years to build a business worth £200,000,000. Five years is roughly 40,000 hours – 40,000 hours to create £200m in value is about £5,000 of value generated per hour. (That's obviously conceived under the false assumption that I did it all myself and that the value of my contribution was consistent throughout.)

When people started paying me large fees per hour, I inevitably started to view the rest of my time through the same monetary lens. If someone's willing to pay me £10,000 per hour, then why am I wasting one hour putting up this shelf, cleaning this carpet or washing my clothes. These are things that I should be spending money on, not time – the time is evidently worth considerably more. I should not be cleaning the carpet; I should pay someone to do it, and place the saved chip on things I intrinsically enjoy like building my company, writing my book, seeing my family, socialising with friends or walking my dog.

In fact, even before I reached this point – where my time became very valuable – I should have treated it as such. I should have avoided time-consuming, low-return tasks and said 'no' as much as possible. That would have brought me to this point sooner and would have made my life intrinsically more rewarding. As the notorious investor and philosopher Naval Ravikant evangelises in the book *The Almanack of Naval Ravikant*:

> No one is going to value you more than you value yourself. You have to set a very high personal hourly rate and you have to stick to it. Even when I was young, I just decided I was worth a lot more than the market thought

I was worth, and I started treating myself that way.

Always factor your time into every decision. How much time does it take? It's going to take you an hour to get across town to get something. If you value yourself at one hundred dollars an hour, that's basically throwing one hundred dollars out of your pocket. Are you going to do that?

Fast forward to your wealthy self and pick some intermediate hourly rate. Set a very high hourly aspirational rate for yourself and stick to it. It should seem and feel absurdly high. If it doesn't, it's not high enough. Whatever you picked, my advice to you would be to raise it.

”

Looking at my own time habits through a monetary framework has helped me to decide what I should and shouldn't be doing. My manager and personal assistant have often witnessed me making decisions based on this framework: 'I shouldn't be doing that', 'someone else can solve that problem' or, as arrogant as it sounds, I'll even say 'my time is more expensive than that'. Again, I'm not saying that to be an arrogant arsehole or because I have delusions of grandeur. I'm saying that because it's my sole responsibility to defend, protect and conserve my time. Nothing matters more, and my time is all I have.

If I can outsource, I will. If I can get a taxi instead of walking in order to allocate more time to an intrinsic goal I will. If I can lend more time to my core goals by hiring a chef or getting a takeaway rather than cooking, I will. This doesn't mean my life is some ultra-optimised, money-driven military process – it's not. It means I'm able to save time on things that I don't truly value to spend more time on the things that I do. To me, this is the truest definition of wealth – someone who has the freedom of time and can spend more of it doing the things that they value. But it's also the most important philosophy behind being happy and successful – spending your time doing what you love, and on what you believe matters.

Of all the advice, stories and anecdotes I've shared in this book it's obvious to me that this chapter is probably the most critical, simple and actionable. How you choose to spend your time is probably the centre point in your circle of influence, therefore changing what you spend your time on can indisputably change your life more than any other single behavioural change.

Complicated self-help jargon aside, if you were able to protect your time a little better, become a little more intentional in how you place your chips on the roulette table of your life and develop more clarity on the things that hold long-term, intrinsic value to you, then you probably wouldn't need to read another self-help personal-development book in your life. At the most fundamental level, this isn't just the most important thing, it's the only thing. It holds the answer to your mental, emotional and spiritual health, and in my life it's proved to be the doorway to becoming the happy sexy millionaire I naively aspired to become.

Time is both free and priceless. The person you are now is a consequence of how you used your time in the past. The person you'll become in the future is a consequence of how you use your time in the present. Spend your time wisely, gamble it intrinsically and save it diligently.

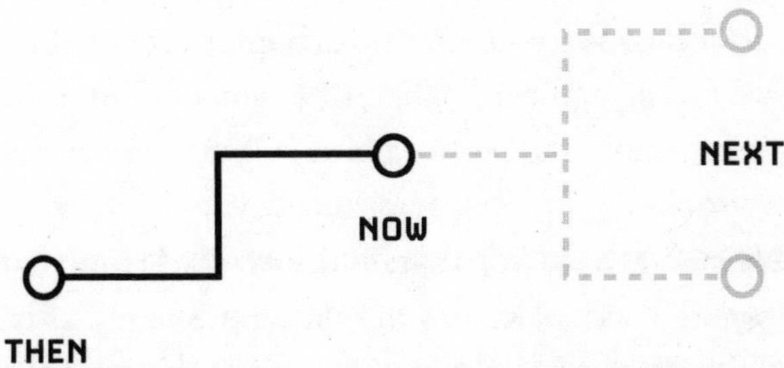

YOUR LIFE RIGHT NOW IS A RESULT OF WHAT YOU DID A YEAR AGO. YOUR LIFE A YEAR FROM NOW WILL BE A RESULT OF WHAT YOU DO RIGHT NOW.

ACT ACCORDINGLY!

Chapter Twenty

MAKING PEACE WITH MY DIARY

REMEMBER ME AT 18 years old, and the list of four things that I wanted scribbled into my diary: a Range Rover, to be a millionaire, to attract women and to be physically attractive?

I wrote these things because I naively believed that being a sexy millionaire was the path to happiness. Now, 10 years later, after becoming a multi-millionaire, buying the car of my dreams, dating beautiful women and meticulously sculpting my body, I'm the sexy millionaire my younger self aspired to become. So, I guess you're wondering how it feels?

AMAZING!

No. Lol. I'm joking.

Relative to how I felt then, even in my toughest moments of stealing pizzas to feed myself and fighting for somewhere to live while being disowned by my family, I don't feel different now. That sounds like nonsensical privileged bullshit, I know. Believe me, I can't believe it either – this wasn't the outcome that my social conditioning promised me. I have no incentive to lie to you – you've already bought my book. I haven't lied to you once in this book and I'm not about to start in the last chapter.

I neither regret my naive aspirations nor admire them. The truth is, they were always too empty to feel anything meaningful when I accomplished them. It's just that I understand that now – I know why I wrote those things and I know what I should have written instead. I know that I was insecure, bruised and seeking validation from the things that had invalidated me as a kid: money, others' opinions and fitting in.

I understand the danger of not bringing my unconscious childhood stories into my conscious control, and I understand that the extrinsic goals I focused on were never going to give me the intrinsic rewards I was seeking. Obviously not.

I had to try to 'fix' myself in order to realise that 'fixing' myself wasn't possible – because nothing was actually broken. I was fine, I was always 'sexy' enough, worthy enough and capable enough of being totally happy – I was already enough. I had wrongly believed a bunch of poorly constructed, poorly evidenced external stories that tried to convince me otherwise – but those stories were wrong.

As a kid, I remember crying on Christmas Day because I didn't have presents, while surrounded by a loving family in a warm home with a generous amount of food on the table. I was so clearly privileged, loved and fortunate.

Still to this day, I regret my naivety and I want to take this opportunity to apologise to my parents for how awful my petulant, ungrateful reaction must have made them feel. I just didn't know better. They gave me everything I needed, but the society I lived in convinced me that it wasn't enough, and that therefore I wasn't enough.

Where did the idea that I didn't have 'enough' come from? What force implanted this in the mind of a young kid who was born in a village in Botswana, Africa? Ironically, it was calling off the search for 'happiness' that made me the happiest

I've ever been; it was the realisation that I was already enough that opened the door to a level of gratitude that had escaped me for my entire life.

It was realising that all of the stories I had believed, that had made me feel broken, inadequate and inferior, weren't true or didn't matter, and relinquishing the self-imposed power I had allowed them to have over me. It was freeing myself from these extrinsic distractions and zero-sum games, that made me more successful. It was no longer craving approval from the opposite sex and being desperate for romantic attention that made me consistent in the gym. It was that stability, and the lack of external validation, that led me to real love.

I became a happy sexy millionaire when I realised that striving to be a happy sexy millionaire was the one thing that stood the greatest chance of stopping me from becoming one.

This, I think is the key to everything. But it almost makes no sense.

HOW CAN I BE ENOUGH, IF I WANT TO BE SO MUCH MORE?

How can you live your life feeling that you are already enough, right now – that you are everything you need to be, while intentionally striving to be so much more? How do you make sense of that contradiction?

The truth is that this question is just a poor use of words crafted by a bunch of societal myths. If you achieve great things, climb the career ladder or become a 'happy sexy millionaire', you don't actually become 'more' than you intrinsically are – you never become 'more', 'superior' or inherently 'better'.

Sometimes you have to call off the search to find everything you've been searching for.

You are you, and you will always be that. Your life doesn't have varying and fluctuating levels of inherent value – despite what social media, pop culture, magazines, adverts and movies might have led you to believe.

You'll never be intrinsically defined, valued or measured by your car, bank balance, job title, followers or accomplishments. That's a socially propagated lie inspired by societal status games, and it's a lie that feels so fucking tempting to believe – especially in the social media age. It's a lie that makes us desire to escape ourselves, fix ourselves or go under the knife to correct ourselves. This toxic lie speaks directly to our self-esteem, our ego and our self-efficacy. After all, if it's true that we can become 'more' than we are right now, we must surely be less.

It's all a fucking lie.
You are enough.
And you always were.

REAL ambition is not based on or inspired by the desire to be 'more' than you are. That isn't real ambition. That's the same insecure pursuit for external validation that I embarked on at 18 years old. Real ambition isn't about 'less' or 'more', status or fame, approval or disapproval. Real ambition is about you; it doesn't care about likes, followers or comments, it cares about what honestly matters to you.

So paradoxically, it's the feeling that you aren't enough that will persuade you to spend your life chasing false external goals down dead ends. And it's realising that you are enough that creates the real genuine ambition to pursue your greatest internal goals, for the sake of nothing more than fulfilment, satisfaction and enjoyment.

You'll never be defined, valued or measured by your car, bank balance, job title, followers or accomplishments.

Being content with who you are and where you are is therefore the driving force for real ambition – not an impairment to it. Knowing that you are already enough will give you the focus, genuine motivation and, therefore, the consistency that you will need to pursue the things that genuinely matter to you, for your own reasons.

And as I said earlier, it's the pursuit of those things, not even the attainment of them, that will give you the happiness we're all so desperately 'searching' for.

You are already enough. This truth is the platform from which to hear your internal voice and to pursue its calling with the genuine desire that you will need to 'become' all that you are destined to be.

You are already enough.

You are already enough.

STEVEN'S READING LIST

1. *Lost Connections* by Johann Hari
2. *Indistractable* by Nir Eyal
3. *The Slight Edge* by Jeff Olsen
4. *The Psychology of Money* by Morgan Housel
5. *The Social Animal* by Elliot Aronson
6. *Elon Musk* by Ashlee Vance
7. *The Ride of a Lifetime* by Robert Iger
8. *Outliers* by Malcolm Gladwell
9. *12 Rules for Life* by Jordan Peterson
10. *The Chimp Paradox* by Professor Steve Peters

WHERE YOU CAN FIND ME

Instagram @steven
Facebook @SteveBartlettShow
YouTube @StevenBartlett
Twitter @SteveBartlettSC
Podcast: The Diary of a CEO

REFERENCES

CHAPTER 2

Peer, M, 'The Optimized Geek – Reboot Your Life' [podcast], hosted by Stephan Spencer, available at: https://marisapeer.com/optimized-geek/

Dorling, D, 'Life expectancy in Britain has stagnated, meaning that a million years of life could disappear by 2058 – why?', available at: https://www.independent.co.uk/voices/uk-life-expectancy-drops-2058-government-cuts-austerity-nhs-national-health-a8131526.html

CHAPTER 3

Liberto, D, 'Relativity trap', Investopedia, 2019, available at: https://www.investopedia.com/terms/r/relativity-trap.asp

CHAPTER 4

Bono, G, Emmons, R A, et al, 'Gratitude in practice and the practice of gratitude', in *Positive Pschology In Practice*, Hoboken, New Jersey: John Wiley & Sons, Inc, 2004

Carmona, C, Buunk, A P, et al, 'Do social comparison and coping play a role in the development of burnout? Cross-sectional and longitudinal findings', *Journal of Occupational and Organizational Psychology*, 79, 85–99, available at: https://bpspsychub.onlinelibrary.wiley.com/doi/abs/10.1348/096317905X40808

Konicki, L, 'Kylie Jenner Reveals Struggle with Anxiety "My Whole

Young Adult Life"', Onecountry.com, 2019, available at: www.onecountry.com/pop-culture/kylie-jenner-message-about-battle-anxiety

Llewellyn Smith, J, 'The selfie doctor', *The Times*, 2017, available at: https://www.thetimes.co.uk/article/the-doctor-who-tweaks-the-faces-of-millennials-3pz6xqwwc

Solon, O, 'Facetune is conquering Instagram, but does it take airbrushing too far?', *Guardian*, 2018, available at: www.theguardian.com/media/2018/mar/09/facetune-photoshopping-app-instagram-body-image-debate?fbclid=IwAR3unUoCIRCE2JKy6LPYCYUtMomSL6eZovO-DpkSBUoPgeoO3xKrxLleWl8

Royal Society For Public Health (RSPH), 'Instagram ranked worst for young people's mental health', 2017, available at: www.rsph.org.uk/about-us/news/instagram-ranked-worst-for-young-people-s-mental-health.html

Williams, B, 'How many tattoos does Kylie Jenner have?', Showbiz Cheatsheet, 2020, available at: www.cheatsheet.com/entertainment/how-many-tattoos-does-kylie-jenner-have.html

CHAPTER 5

Bono, G, Emmons, R A, et al, 'Gratitude in practice and the practice of gratitude', in *Positive Pschology In Practice*, Hoboken, New Jersey: John Wiley & Sons, Inc, 2004

Healthbeat column, 'Giving thanks can make you healthier', Harvard Medical School, (n.d.), available at: www.health.harvard.edu/health-beat/giving-thanks-can-make-you-happier

Chaplin, L, John, D R, et al, 'The impact of gratitude on adolescent materialism and generosity', *The Journal of Positive Psychology*, 2018, 14, 1–10, available at: https://doi.org/10.1080/17439760.2018.1497688

Donnelly, G, Zheng, T, Haisley, E, and Norton, M, 'The Amount and Source of Millionaires' Wealth (Moderately) Predicts Their Happiness', *Personality and Social Psychology Bulletin*, 2018, 44: 5, available at: www.hbs.edu/faculty/Publication%20Files/donnelly%20zheng%20haisley%20norton_26bec744-c924-4a28-8439-5a74abe9c8da.pdf

Hawkes, K, O'Connell, J, et al, 'Hunter-gatherer studies and human evolution: A very selective review.' *American Journal of Physical Anthropology*, 2018, 165(4), 777–800, available at: https://doi.org/10.1002/ajpa.23403

Hsieh, N, 'A Global Perspective on Religious Participation and Suicide' *Journal of Health and Social Behavior*, 2017, available at: https://doi.org/10.1177/0022146517715896

Morin, A, '7 scientifically proven benefits of gratitude that will motivate you to give thanks year-round', *Forbes*, 2014, available at: www.forbes.com/sites/amymorin/2014/11/23/7-scientifically-proven-benefits-of-gratitude-that-will-motivate-you-to-give-thanks-year-round/?sh=6bb1c10183c0

Patterson Neubert, A, 'Money only buys happiness for a certain amount', Purdue University, 2018, available at: www.purdue.edu/newsroom/releases/2018/Q1/money-only-buys-happiness-for-a-certain-amount.html

Pinsker, J, 'The reason many ultrarich people aren't satisfied with their wealth', *The Atlantic*, 2018, available at: www.theatlantic.com/family/archive/2018/12/rich-people-happy-money/577231

Seligman, M, *Flourish: A visionary new understanding of happiness and well-being*, New York: Atria Paperback, 2011

Smith, T W, 'Job Satisfaction in the United States', NORC/University of Chicago, 2007, available at: www-news.uchicago.edu/releases/07/pdf/070417.jobs.pdf

CHAPTER 6

Eferighe, J, 'Is it becoming okay to cheat? Millennials are doing it more than ever', The Social Man, (n.d.), available at: https://thesocialman.com/becoming-okay-cheat-millennials/

Semeuels, A, 'We Are All Accumulating Mountains of Things', *The Atlantic*, available at: https://www.theatlantic.com/technology/archive/2018/08/online-shopping-and-accumulation-of-junk/567985/

CHAPTER 7

'Follow Your Passion' image plotted using The Google Ngram Viewer.

Haas, A P, Eliason, M, et al, 'Suicide and suicide risk in lesbian, gay, bisexual, and transgender populations: review and recommendations', *J Homosex.*, 2011, 58(1):10–51, available at: doi:10.1080/00918369.2011.534038

May, C, 'Meaningful work can be something you grow into, not something you discover', Scientific American, 2018, https://www.scientificamerican.com/article/life-advice-dont-find-your-passion/

Semuels, A, 'We are all accumulating mountains of things', *The Atlantic*, 2018, available at: https://www.theatlantic.com/technology/archive/2018/08/online-shopping-and-accumulation-of-junk/567985/

CHAPTER 9

Barker, E, 'Why are we so bad at predicting what will make us happy?', Business Insider, 2011, available at: www.businessinsider.com/why-are-we-so-bad-at-predicting-what-will-make-us-happy-2011-8?r=US&IR=T

Bolles, R N, *What Color is Your Parachute?*, Berkeley, California: Ten Speed Press, 1960

Keller, G and Papasan, J, *The One Thing*, Portland, Oregon: Bard Press, 2012

Corporation for National and Community Service, 'The Health Benefits of Volunteering: A review of recent research', Office of Research and Policy Development, Washington DC, 2007, available at: www.nationalservice.gov/pdf/07_0506_hbr.pdf

Diener, E and Biswas-Diener, R, 'Will Money Increase Subjective Well-Being? A Literature Review and Guide to Needed Research', The Science of Wellbeing, 2009, available at: https://doi.org/10.1007/978-90-481-2350-6_6

Doll, K, 'What is Peak End Theory? A psychologist explains how our memory fools us', PositivePsychology.com, 2020, https://positivepsychology.com/what-is-peak-end-theory

Gallup, G, 'Human Needs and Satisfactions: A Global Survey', *The Public Opinion Quarterly,* 1976, 40(4), 459–467, available at: www.jstor.org/stable/2748277

Ganster, D and Rosen, C, 'Work Stress and Employee Health: A Multidisciplinary Review', *Journal of Management,* 2013, 39, 1085-1122, available at: https://doi.org/10.1177%2F0149206313475815

Gerhart, B and Fang, M, 'Pay, Intrinsic Motivation, Extrinsic Motivation, Performance, and Creativity in the Workplace: Revisiting Long-Held Beliefs.' *Annual Review of Organizational Psychology and Organizational Behavior,* 2015, available at: https://doi.org/10.1146/annurev-orgpsych-032414-111418

Gilbert, D, *Stumbling on Happiness,* New York: Alfred A. Knopf, 2006

Kierkegaard, S, *The Sickness Unto Death* [Penguin Classics], New York: Penguin, 1989

Society for Human Resource Management, 'Employee Job Satisfaction and Engagement', 2016, available at: www.shrm.org/hr-today/trends-and-forecasting/research-and-surveys/Documents/2016-Employee-Job-Satisfaction-and-Engagement-Report.pdf

Smith, T, 'Job Satisfaction in the United States', available at: https://study.sagepub.com/system/files/gss_codebook.pdf

Tatar, A and Nesip Ogun, M, *Impact of Job Satisfaction on Organizational Commitment,* LAP LAMBERT Academic Publishing: Saarbrücken, Germany, 2019

'Top Occupations in Job Satisfaction Chart' image by Smith, T, 'Job Satisfaction in the United States', available at: https://study.sagepub.com/system/files/gss_codebook.pdf

CHAPTER 10

Breslow, J, 'What does solitary confinement do to your mind?', PBS, 2014, available at https://www.pbs.org/wgbh/frontline/article/what-does-solitary-confinement-do-to-your-mind/

Ferdowsian, H R, et al, 'Signs of mood and anxiety disorders in chim panzees', *PloS One*, 2011, 6(6) e19855, available at: https://doi.org/10.1371/journal.pone.0019855

Hadaway, P F, Alexander, B K, et al, 'The effect of housing and gender on preference for morphine-sucrose solutions in rats', *Psychopharmacology*, 1979, 66, 87–91, available at: https://doi.org/10.1007/BF00431995

Hari, J, *Lost Connections: Uncovering the Real Causes of Depression – and the Unexpected Solutions*, London: Bloomsbury Publishing, 2018

Jarvis, H, 'Generation lonely: Millennials loneliest age group', 2018, Brunel University London, available at: https://www.brunel.ac.uk/news-and-events/news/articles/Generation-lonely

Murthy, V, 'Work and the loneliness epidemic', *Harvard Business Review*, 2017, available at: https://hbr.org/2017/09/work-and-the-loneliness-epidemic

Peele, S, image extracted from 'The Meaning of addiction', Lexington, Mass, USA, 1985, pp.77-96

Polak, E, 'New Cigna study reveals loneliness at epidemic levels in America', 2018, Cigna, available at: www.cigna.com/newsroom/news-releases/2018/new-cigna-study-reveals-loneliness-at-epidemic-levels-in-america

Rico-Uribe, L. A., Caballero, F. F. et al, 'Association of loneliness with all-cause mortality: A meta-analysis', *PloS One*, 2018, 13(1), e0190033, available at: https://doi.org/10.1371/journal.pone.0190033-

Roberts, N, 'Americans sit more than anytime in history and it's literally killing us', *Forbes*, 2019, available at: https://www.forbes.com/sites/nicolefisher/2019/03/06/americans-sit-more-than-anytime-in-history-and-its-literally-killing-us/?sh=1f7746b7779

Seay, B, Alexander, B K, et al, 'Maternal behavior of socially deprived Rhesus monkeys', *The Journal of Abnormal and Social Psychology, 1964,* 69(4), 345–354, available at: https://doi.org/10.1037/h0040539

The Week staff, 'An epidemic of loneliness', *The Week*, 2019, available at: https://theweek.com/articles/815518/epidemic-loneliness

UK Government, 'Policy Paper: A Connected Society: a strategy for tackling loneliness', 2018, available at: www.gov.uk/government/publications/a-connected-society-a-strategy-for-tackling-loneliness

CHAPTER 11

Adolphs, R, 'The social brain: neural basis of social knowledge', *Annual Review of Psychology*, 2009, 60, 693–716, available at: https://doi.org/10.1146/annurev.psych.60.110707.163514

Bradberry, T, '11 ways emotionally intelligent people overcome uncertainty', (n.d.), available at: www.talentsmart.com/articles/11-Ways-Emotionally-Intelligent-People-Overcome-Uncertainty-1596789451-p-1.html

Dunning, D, Johnson, K, et al, 'Why People Fail to Recognize Their Own Incompetence', *Current Directions in Psychological Science*, 2003, 12(3):83–87, available at: https://psycnet.apa.org/doi/10.1111/1467-8721.01235

CHAPTER 14

Clear, J, *Atomic Habits* New York: Avery, 2018

Eyal, N, *Indistractable*, Dallas, Texas: Benbella Books, 2019

'Life/Time' image from https://wisdom-trek.com/resources

Miller, J, 'Opinion: This Warren Buffett rule can work wonders on your portfolio', Market Watch, 2015, available at: www.marketwatch.com/story/this-warren-buffett-rule-can-work-wonders-on-your-portfolio-2016-04-26

Norcross, J, Mrykalo, M, et al, 'Auld Lang Syne: Success Predictors, Change Processes, and Self-Reported Outcomes of New Year's Resolvers and Nonresolvers', *Journal of Clinical Psychology*, 2002, 58: 397–405, available at: https://doi.org/10.1002/jclp.1151

'Total Savings' image from investor.gov

CHAPTER 15

Job, V, Dweck, C S, et al, 'Ego Depletion—Is It All in Your Head?: Implicit Theories About Willpower Affect Self-Regulation', *Psychological Science*, 2010, 21(11): 1686–1693, available at: https://doi.org/10.1177/0956797610384745

CHAPTER 16

Galvin, B, Randel, A, et al, 'Changing the Focus of Locus (of Control): A targeted review of the locus of control literature and agenda for future research', *Journal of Organizational Behavior*, 2018, 39: 7, 820–833, available at: https://doi.org/10.1002/job.2275

Grelot, M C, 'Gender Differences in the Relation Between Locus of Control and Physiological Responses', Master of Science (MS), thesis, Psychology, Old Dominion University, 1989, available at: at: https://doi.org/10.25777/jq08-g161

Internal/External Locus of Control Chart by US psychologist Julian B Rotter, 1916-2014

CHAPTER 17

Deci, E, 'The Effects of Externally Mediated Rewards on Intrinsic Motivation', *Journal of Personality and Social Psychology*, 1971, 18, 105–115, available at: https://doi.org/10.1037/h0030644

Deci, E and Ryan, R M, '*Self-determination theory', 2012,* published in *Handbook of Theories of Social Psychology* [Ed. Van Lange, P A M, et al], Sage Publications Ltd, available at: https://doi.org/10.4135/9781446249215.n216

Niemiec, C P, Ryan, R M, et al, 'The Path Taken: Consequences of attaining intrinsic and extrinsic aspirations in post-college life', *Journal of Research in Personality*, 2009, 73(3), 291–306, available at: https://doi.org/10.016/j.jrp.2008.09.001

Ware, B, *The Top Five Regrets of the Dying*, **New York: Hay House, Inc, 2011**

CHAPTER 18

Adams, S, *How To Fail at Almost Everything and Still Win Big: Kind of the story of my life,* New York: Portfolio/Penguin, 2013

Isaacson, W, *Steve Jobs,* New York: Simon & Schuster, 2011

Skill stack image by Thomas Pueyo

CHAPTER 19

'What is Death Café?', https://deathcafe.com/what/

Jobs, S, Commencement address delivered on June 12, 2005, available at: https://news.stanford.edu/2005/06/14/jobs-061505/

Ravikant,N, *The Almanack of Naval Ravikant: A guide to wealth and happiness,* Magrathea Publishing, 2020

Seneca, *On the Shortness of Life* [Translated by J W Basore], Loeb Classical Library London: William Heinemann, 1932

ACKNOWLEDGEMENTS

To all of those that have supported my journey, this book and my life.

Sophie Chapman
Dominic Murray
Adrian Sington
Lauren Whelan
Holly Whitaker
Kate Latham
Rebecca Mundy
Caitriona Horne
Matthew Everett
Giuliana Caranante
Sarah Christie
Dominic Gribben
Anne Newman
Jane Smith
Jack Sylvester
Ashley Jones
Dominic McGregor
Anthony Logan
Michael Heaven
Oliver Yonchev

Holger Hansen
Christian Grobel
Wanja S. Oberhof
Andrew 'Doddz' Evans
Melanie Lopes
Kiera Lawlor
Nick Speakman
Hannah Anderson
Cathal 'Catty' Berragan
Merle Driver
Samuel Budd
Katie Wallwork
Lisa Sayers
Katy Leeson
Paul Stevens
Steph Ledigo
Richard Dash
Lianne Foran
Montarna Atkinson
Ellie Cheadle
Ellis Duke
Alex Ayin
Leanne Ayin
Peter Daly
Richard Johnson
Marc Nohr
Julian Hearn
Shakil Khan

Thank you x